WHAT OTHERS ARE SAYING ABOUT
"The Art of Self-Healing"

One must walk the long journey in the spiritual realms in order to deliver profound multi-dimensional healing in a practical, ready to use form. This gift of great teachers is exactly what Julie Lewin demonstrates throughout this book. She gives amazing, easy to apply healing tools to help you heal from the inside out.

Julie's inspirational personal story makes this type of self-healing accessible to everyone. You will have fun doing the exercises and at the same time experience deep healing and transformation. So clever Julie – it is a wonderful way to help us all step into our intuition and healing.

The exceptional results Julie's techniques are producing is a big motivation to apply them all. This is new medicine! It is new multi-dimensional healing on all levels and by reading this book you will take the first step into becoming an apprentice of an amazing intuitive healer and teacher of your age.

Dr Lea Imsiragic, M.Sci – Author "A Handbook of Energy Astrology", Business Astrology and Astro-Medicine

৪০ ૯૪

Julie Lewin has found her way to ancient wisdom through dedicated practice of a natural talent in much the same way a concert pianist earns applause while the rest of us fumble over scales. This book resonates with her voice and contains the gift of her "templates" giving us the opportunity to practice the quantum jump into the music of our souls, and become better conductors of the symphony we call our bodies.

Cathie Hill, Author "The Ripple Effect of Being: A Thought Experiment"

৪০ ૯૪

WHAT OTHERS ARE SAYING ABOUT MEDICAL INTUITION WITH JULIE

12 Years Of Pain Almost Gone In Weeks

To work with Julie Lewin has been life-transforming. Severe and virtually chronic pain I had for twelve years has almost disappeared in a few weeks ... The treatment combined her intuitive healing abilities, which are extraordinary, with the guided visualisation she has asked me to do. These visualisations were easy and yet remarkably powerful.

Maryanne Sea, Holistic Practitioner, Perth, Australia

Julie's Accuracy Is Uncanny

Being with Julie is like being in the presence of angels. You leave feeling full of grace, enlightenment and purity. Julie's accuracy is uncanny. Her consultations provide guidance and clarity in relation to health and life path. Her answers were needed and appreciated.

Sandra Rodman, Company Director, Brisbane, Australia

Doctor wrote "Amazed, Mysterious and Magic"

From Monday when I first spoke to you, I started to do things that I hadn't done for a long time. [Three days after talking to you] I went to see my chest specialist who was amazed at my progress and recovery. He wrote in his report to my GP, AMAZED, MYSTERIOUS and MAGIC. I have never in my life tried anything like this. I am by nature a skeptic and I hope this will convince you of how desperate I was to go to these lengths

Dennis K., Melbourne, Australia

I Was So Impressed!

I really wanted to say congratulations. I was so impressed with your workshop. I feel just wonderful in spite of the oedema hanging around. Each day on our holiday I could feel myself improving and the same applies to since I have been home. I feel really, really well, which is so fantastic. It's been a long time.

Lola, Cancer Patient, Sydney, Australia

the art of self-healing

HEALING SECRETS OF WORLD FAMOUS MEDICAL INTUITIVE JULIE LEWIN

CELESTIAL
CONSCIOUSNESS
PUBLISHING

DISCLAIMER

All the information, techniques, skills and concepts contained within this publication are of the nature of general comment only and are not in any way recommended as individual advice. The intent is to offer a variety of information to provide a wider range of choices now and in the future, recognising that we all have widely diverse circumstances and viewpoints. Should any reader choose to make use of the information contained herein, this is their decision, and the contributors (and their companies), authors and publishers do not assume any responsibilities whatsoever under any condition or circumstances. It is recommended the reader obtain their own independent advice.

First publication of Chapter 5 published in "Your Well-Being Sorted!" edited by Kizzi Nkwocha as co-contributor.

First publication of Master Cell Meditation in "Life Sucks but You Can Turn It Around" by Maree Hamilton as co-contributor

Copyright © 2015 by Julie Lewin

All rights reserved. No part of this publication may be reproduced, stored in a retrieval system, or transmitted in any form or by any means, electronic mechanical, photocopying, recording or otherwise, without the prior written permission from the publisher.

Cover Design and Formatting: Tash Lewin

National Library of Australia

Cataloguing-in-Publication entry:

Lewin, Julie, 1959-

The Art of Self-Healing / Julie Lewin

2nd ed. Previously known as AreekeerA ® Vibration: Healing Yourself From Within

Incudes bibliographical references

ISBN: 978-0-9874957-1-6

1. Intuition. 2. Healing. 3. Metaphysics. 4. Self-Help. 5. Quantum.

Published by Celestial Consciousness Publishing

PO Box 1142, Milton BC Qld 4064

Email: support@julielewin.com

Phone: +61 421 542 436

DEDICATION

My amazing family and friends
Your support means everything

Our extraordinary and trusting clients
Without you this wisdom would not
have been downloaded

ACKNOWLEDGMENTS

What an extraordinary adventure it has been to write this book. I started writing in October 2010 – however, it wasn't smooth sailing. I struggled to find my writing groove and the words simply wouldn't flow.

I put it aside until November 2012. It was a group of special women – Angelique Adams, Belinda Hayward, Di Crane, Fiona Gibson and Irene Christie – who attended my second intuitive healing retreat at the beginning of November who inspired me to finish it – THANK YOU.

And a huge thank you to the 5 special women who attended my first retreat in April 2012 for their courage, faith and trust in my ability to turn my dream and vision into an exceptional reality – Assisi Chant, Donna Williams, Macky Steele Scott, Mukhand-Jeet Kaur and Nika Mundell. Without your trust in me to deliver untested material and allow your transformations to unfold so radically, I may not have continued with these retreats nor shared my metaphysical and spiritual adventure with others. Thank you for your continued love, friendship, encouragement and support.

It's been an honour and privilege to explore beyond the boundaries of ordinary man to bring you a different way of living in the new Age.

Without a supportive family, achievements such as this are not possible.

My thanks to you cannot be measured, BIG HUGS and GRATITUDE to my awesome husband and best friend Frank, our amazing children Natasha and Tristan and my extra special Mum who has listened to and encouraged my extraordinary life without reservation.

A HUGE thank you to all my amazing mentors, friends and clients! Your support over the last 30 years has made this project possible. Without you these adventures wouldn't have been lived and the words wouldn't have been written.

Lynika Cruz, kindred spirit - it is not often you meet someone who totally gets you – feels you – communicates with you multi-dimensionally – and you know they truly know you. The gift of you in my life is a blessing. THANK YOU for writing the Foreword for this book.

A very special THANK YOU to my doctors and health and wellness support team. Without your invaluable assistance, I would not be here today to share this wisdom. I am immensely grateful.

And lastly, a HUGE THANK YOU to Lynne McGee for starting this adventure back in 1984. Without your insight and gift, I don't know how my life would have played out

CONTENTS

Foreword

Preface

Introduction

1. How To Cleanse Your Energy...15
2. How To Protect Your Energy...23
3. How To Rejuvenate Your Energy..37
4. Creative and Spontaneous Visualisation..47
5. Your Metaphysical Body Language Helps You Heal Yourself..........53
6. How Do You Know If You Are Psychic?..69
7. Develop Your Psychic & Intuitive Gifts..77
8. How Insight and Intuition Can Help...81
9. 8 Key Qualities of Intuitive Insight..95
10. The Rules of Vibrational Healing?..129
11. Where does Illness or Disease Begin?..137
12. Unique Healing Templates..165
13. Where to Now?..197

FOREWORD

My own relationship with intuition is a fiercely strong one.

It's no wonder *The Art of Self-Healing* resonated so clearly with me. Julie Lewin has created a much needed, timely and valuable book on a topic that will enable you to change your life for the better in powerful ways.

I have great adversity to thank for the immense strength and dexterity forged within my own intuition. It gifted me a deep and trusted relationship with myself.

As a child abandoned to the street at an early age, barely 14 years old, if I hadn't developed an intense trust in my own intuition, and myself, I shudder to think what my life may look like today. In fact there's a very high chance I wouldn't be alive at all, sitting at my desk right now, writing this foreword.

Surviving the streets is no easy feat; coming out of it with a positive, self-sustainable outlook is even less likely. Add to that the weight of being a young, female child and the odds of surviving intact, lessen considerably.

I'd scuttle up trees at night to avoid danger and snatch at sleep; sometimes I'd take my chances under parked railway carriages to try and avoid the rains. Strangers, rats, mice, cockroaches, insects, spiders all share the same aim and I encountered them up close, constantly. My intuition was on full alert at all times.

As a street child, there's rarely a warm, safe, comfortable place to hide for long, if at all.

Eating was another seemingly impossible task for a homeless child but not one you can ignore. At some point you must eat, I survived mostly on navigating the scene and trusting my hunches, scavenging for old bread every few days or so from the back of bakeries for almost a year.

Danger comes thick and frequently on the streets, in many guises, particularly to a young girl. I can't count the amount of times my intuition and self-trust either got me out of a pending situation or managed to head it off, at the pass, through trusting what my 'gut' told me. Which street and group to avoid at a particular time, when to get out of a place fast and run, which tree to climb for a little reprieve etc.

I was fortunate in the irony that a traumatic, violent and turbulent earlier childhood had gifted me with exactly what I would need on the streets. Early home life skilled me in developing an inner knowing, an awareness that spoke to me often. Fortunately for me, I listened to it.

I didn't really know another way. I experienced inner isolation a lot at home as it wasn't a safe place to communicate with others, interaction meant danger. You kept your distance and tried as hard as you could to avoid the inevitable onslaught of abuse. I was my best friend and confidante.

Listening to myself was my best tool and my connection to my intuition became intensely powerful. It guided me through extreme adversity to the phenomenal life I have today.

The Art of Self-Healing is a welcome and timely breakthrough in describing and illustrating the immense gift and power of intuition. However, the wealth of this book doesn't stop there.

Having a deep connection with yourself and your own inner knowing is the key to success and fortitude in all areas of life. In simplistic yet refreshingly engaging terms, Julie Lewin has managed to describe the craft of accessing our own intuition and how we too can utilize it for our own wellbeing, how to employ it for diagnosis of disease and other health ailments.

Julie guides the reader with deeply valuable lessons and intriguing examples. Through her captivating book woven with case studies and her own incredible, personal journey, we soon see how each of us can access and develop this innate gift of intuition.

Through Julie's honesty and down to earth wisdom, we come to see how each of us can apply specific, step-by-step techniques to propel us toward healing. We also learn how we can help others, be it friends, family or clients, through developing our relationship with intuition and its many gifts.

In the years I have personally known Julie, I have witnessed her warmth and calm energy, along with gifted patience and passion at helping others. Julie has an innate gift of being able to teach with both authenticity and pizazz.

Pizazz may seem an unusual word to describe a healer, but it is this exact kind of 'alive' energy that lets us know, Julie truly walks the walk. She manages to infuse enthusiasm and encouragement throughout her book, which keeps the reader turning page after page.

The Art of Self-Healing teaches us the gift of intuition is the birth right of all of us. Julie has done a superb job of laying the stepping-stones out one by one, so we too can move forward and benefit from a renewed and accessible sense of empowerment in our lives.

Despite enormous odds, developing and listening to my own intuition not only saved my life, it set me up for a phenomenal and extraordinary life.

The Art of Self-Healing will guide you to discover your own intrinsic gift of intuition. I'm excited to see this book become available, it will be a powerhouse to those ready to take their health and lives to a whole new level of freedom and success.

Dr Lynika Cruz – Author of "Beggars *CAN* Be Choosers"
www.lynika.com

PREFACE

Are you satisfied with your level of health and wellbeing? If not, you should be. You don't need to suffer from poor health. You can help yourself!

How? This book will show you how. You have the ability to intuitively find the root cause of all disease. Right now you may not be aware that you have this ability, but you do.

The gift of intuition is the birth right of every man and woman and it lies hidden within you just waiting to be awakened.

The secret to bringing your gifts into consciousness is to take action. Just reading about it being possible simply isn't enough.

This book will inspire you to take action – you won't be able to help yourself because the results are so exciting. Each chapter has exercises for you to practice and the results will speak for themselves.

This book does not offer all the solutions for you – no book or course can do that. However, it will open you up to some extraordinary tried and tested techniques, templates and strategies for getting to the root cause of any health and wellness challenges you face. You will be shown a system that will become the foundation for your unique self-healing journey.

This intuitive healing toolbox has been developed over 30 years. These resources have helped thousands of people around the world.

This book has been written to inspire you to transform your health and wellness yourself. You'll quickly discover how easily you can implement these healing resources.

The win for you is an extraordinary life of health and wellness. The win for me is knowing these tools and healing templates that have taken so long to develop are passed onto as many people as possible.

By following the simple and easy instructions, combined with regular, consistent practice you'll activate and develop your innate intuitive gift. In fact, over time you will find the process of intuitive self-care becomes second nature to you. It's similar to learning a new language.

You will get the most out of these tools when you are comfortable with the process.

By following the instructions, you too will learn the craft of intuitively locating the root cause of disease and discomfort for yourself.

You will discover that the step-by-step guidelines make it seem very easy. However, it is important you understand the depth and ultimate healing consequences of these seemingly simple templates and techniques.

You will learn about what is possible and what has been done by ordinary people who had no thought of having a special gift. They have been able to follow these instructions and achieve extraordinary results. If they can do it you can do it, too.

However, believing you can do it is not the only thing you have to do, effort is required as well. When you make a cake you need the ingredients, you take action and then after a while the cake is cooked and ready to eat.

It's the same with intuitive healing. In this book you have the tools and the templates. Practice and use them and then the results are achieved.

In the following chapters these templates and healing strategies are explained in detail and the intuitive healing secrets are revealed.

I hope you achieve great success in your life and I look forward to meeting you in person one day soon.

Enjoy!

To Your Health & Wellness

Julie Lewin

Medical Intuitive | Author | Teacher | Mentor

INTRODUCTION

A psychic reading changed my life! In one hour, my world flipped initiating an extraordinary journey into the sacred arts of metaphysical science, spirituality and healing.

Before The Story Begins

I was born on a little farm near Gympie, Queensland, Australia. It was a very difficult pregnancy and even though I was born full term, I was only 2.6kg (5lb 12oz).

The eyes tell an amazing story – mine say I was born with a weak constitution and my health was always going to be a challenge because the building blocks were not strong. With persistence, determination and inexplicable drive, I've turned this weakness into my greatest strength – intuition.

As children we moved around quite a bit; at 4 we moved to Cairns in far north Queensland and I started school there. At 6, we travelled Australia in a caravan. Mum and Dad picked fruit and vegetables where they could and we went to school wherever we happened to be. In grade 2, I went to 9 different schools.

In 1966, we moved to Mount Isa - a copper, silver, lead and zinc mining town in central Australia. It is about 100km from the Queensland / Northern Territory border. Mum convinced Dad to settle down till we all finished school. Even living here, I went to 5 different schools in 11 years before finishing my education.

I've lived in over 30 houses and had over 50 jobs.

We travelled extensively as a family and at 16 I started travelling on my own – including the United States, Canada, Australia, Singapore, Taiwan, Ireland, and Thailand. Sometimes I travelled by myself - an amazing experience which I highly recommend - while other times I travelled with friends and family.

I often wonder whether moving around so much and going to so many different schools as a child prepared me for taking risks and exploring my inner and outer worlds in such depth.

Sometimes we cannot fathom why something happens and it is only later in life we understand the value of those experiences.

Where The Story Begins

My life is about the way of faith and trust.

Since my first memory of divinity at 5, I've been on a journey (sometimes ordinary and sometimes extraordinary) searching for a way to reconnect with God (the Divine Spark).

I use the word God in this book because it is what I use in my day to day life. If you don't like this word because it brings up religious resistance, replace the word God for a word you feel comfortable with that represents the Divine Spark to you.

It first happened in a tiny Methodist church in Freshwater, Cairns after Sunday school. It was a timber church with one door at the front protected from the weather by a portico. Inside there were beautifully polished timber pews inviting seekers to sit. The church was a bit musty inside as if it didn't get enough fresh air and sunlight.

Introduction

This particular Sunday the kids from Sunday school were allowed into church to witness a baptism. We were told to sit quietly in the back and behave ourselves. The congregation started singing the song "Royal Telephone". These are the words that have stuck with me for the last 50 years:

> Telephone to glory, oh, what joy divine!
>
> I can feel the current moving on the line.
>
> Made by God the Father for His very own,
>
> You may talk to Jesus on this royal telephone.

My imagination was captured by these words and the tune. But this wasn't the thing that changed my life in that moment. The angle of the sun was such that just as this song was sung, bright sunlight streamed through the open door creating an arc of light in the dim hall right beside me. Dust particles danced in the sunlight, seemingly to the rhythm of the music.

Everything slowed down and I felt as if the room breathed me, rather than I breathe as a separate being in the room. The dust particles, the sound, the light, the message, the rhythm, the joy all combined - I felt conscious as everything in the room. My little body and being filled with awe and wonder at the mystery of all that is and the search began to experience that connection again.

As a seeker, I've experienced great happiness, love, pleasure, and achievement; and on the flipside I've experienced deep dark unhappiness, betrayal, felt unloved, unattractive, not worthy, isolated, lonely, depressed, and created many health challenges. I've made many miss-takes (as my good friend Maddi calls them) and learned many lessons.

The powerful awakening of my intuition began when my daughter was 7 months old in 1984.

It was then that a friend, Lynne McGee, came to visit and said, *"Julie you are going to see Brother William – an aura reader."*

"I don't think so."

"Oh yes, I think so!"

I was terrified. This intense fear sent waves of adrenalin rushing through my body over and over – it was exhausting. I had no money was my first excuse and Lynne said, *"I'm paying, I'm driving you, I'll look after Natasha, and you're doing it."*

I found out later that Lynne didn't have the money to spare either – that's how important she felt this was for me. It was an incredible gift.

The reading was very frightening.

It triggered my first experience of transfiguration which is when you look at someone eye-to-eye and within 1-2 minutes you start seeing different faces pass over the other person's face. It is as if the outer world is stripped away and their other incarnations reveal themselves.

If you continue to look into the other person's eyes longer than a few minutes you may start to see their clothes transform into period dress as well. It is a fascinating experience. But as you'll find not one that adds any real importance or value to the inner journey.

Anyway, Br William told me of two destinies – the current one and an alternative one.

Current Destiny

This marriage will fail, you will remarry quickly, that marriage will fail, you will be very ill in your 30s and 40s, you will have very few happy moments and die at 53.

I recognized the shocking truth in the first half of the reading and was relieved to hear there was an alternative:-

Alternative Destiny

This marriage will survive, you will overcome illness in your 30s and 40s, you will have many happy moments, and most importantly you have a special gift of x-ray vision. You can see inside people's bodies. If you choose this destiny you will be of great benefit to the world and will live into your 90s.

Whether what Br William said was true or not doesn't matter. What matters is I believed it to be truth!

I knew in my heart if I went down the road of no purpose, no passion, and no map to guide me, I wouldn't cope with that life. I was already planning to leave my husband.

I said to Br William, *"Let's assume I take this new path. How do I do this?"*

He put his hands in the air and said, *"I don't know. I'm just the messenger."*

He told me I could see inside of people's bodies.

Now, back in the early 1980s there wasn't such a term as a "Medical Intuitive", nor any teachers to teach me, so I experimented. I would lie in bed at night and say to God, *"You want me to do this work for you, show me how!"*

I made a lot of miss-takes. I didn't know I needed to protect and cleanse my energy, or refill my inner reservoir regularly. I didn't know that in my search for Divinity I would travel "out there" and take the Divine essence out of my body leaving it vulnerable to disease.

The true path to Happiness is to be Happy and to connect with Source (Divinity). It is an inner journey not an adventure "out there". I learned this lesson the hard way almost dying in the process.

Two Lives

I led a conventional life in the outside world; work and social interaction and a very unconventional life in my inner world.

In 1987, I joined a psychic development group in Brisbane under the leadership of Rev. Marilyn O'Sullivan. We learned how to perform psychometry (pick up energy vibration/messages from objects eg., jewellery), channel, read auras and experience telepathy. As a group, we practiced every week for 2 years. I honed my psychic ability with this group.

The Art of Self-Healing

Psychic ability is different to intuition. I have a very clear distinction on this.

The psychic realm operates at a different vibration to intuition. Yes, it is interesting to have psychic ability, but you also want to hone your intuition which is more instinctive and autonomic.

Note: with psychic information, it is important to be careful how you deliver the information you receive. As you have read in this book, the aura reader told me about two life paths. I believed in the second destiny because I needed to have hope and faith in the opportunity for a better life.

In the guise of helping people through psychic means, clairvoyants deliver messages they believe are real. However, if these messages are not delivered with sensitivity they can play on and loop in the mind of the person receiving the message causing upset, sleep deprivation and mental instability.

Sometimes people manifest what the psychic tells them because it becomes so much a part of their thoughts it resonates as a truth and life decisions are made based on this information.

We are the captain of our own ship. We make choices moment to moment every day about how to live our life. There is nothing right or wrong about the decisions made, they are choices made with ensuing consequences. You determine whether they are "good" or "bad" – yet simply put "it is".

Have you seen the movie "Sliding Doors" with Gwyneth Paltrow? It's about how your life can take a different direction based on whether in a moment you make one decision or another.

The principle of this movie mirrors life.

Makes me curious – are there millions of parallel worlds we live triggered by our choices in each moment? Hmmm, something to ponder isn't it?

Although in saying this, there is a phenomenon I have experienced that tells me perhaps there are milestones we have agreed to prior to birth. Several times in a dark room at night, I've seen a 3-D vision like a coloured holographic movie in the middle of the room with my eyes open. Four or five years later I visit the place I had seen in the vision.

Apparently, this means you are on track. You're on your path. I was happy to discover this description.

Don't attribute other meanings to these experiences, it simply means you are on track and recognise them as a signpost guiding your way.

The Secret To Exceptional Intuition

Practice something metaphysical or spiritual every day, even if it is for 5 minutes. Although, you might find you spend hours some days enjoying this deep dive into the quantum world.

I didn't know I could see inside the body. I don't feel I was born with a special gift. However, I did want a different life to the first one outlined by Br William and took up this option as if my life depended on it. To awaken my intuition I practiced, practiced and practiced some more.

Perhaps my life did depend on it!

Have you ever wondered how an Olympian becomes an elite athlete and wins gold? The secret is in the **Olympian mindset**:

- determination
- inner strength
- hardworking | persistence
- self-motivation
- dealing with adversity | tenaciousness
- optimism and positivity
- strong focus

I have these qualities, too.

School Lesson

I went to a small Catholic high school in Mount Isa called San Jose. At the beginning of Grade 9, I remember being told that because it was a small school every girl had to learn typing.

I did <u>NOT</u> want to be a typist! I wanted to be a nurse!

They said, *"Too bad! You're studying typing. You can study the sciences, but you are learning to type as well."*

At the start of my first typing lesson, I walked into the classroom and saw my new teacher sitting in front of an IBM selectric golf ball typewriter typing at 90 words per minute. Her fingers flew across the typewriter keys.

In that moment I was pierced through the heart and I made a decision *"One day, I will type that fast, too".*

I sat down in front of my clunky manual typewriter and started the laborious process of learning to type. "asdf ;lkj" - I wanted to be the best. Nobody said *"Julie you should be the best!"* I just wanted to be the best!

I knew I had to practice if I wanted a typing speed of 90 words per minute. So I created an invisible typewriter on my lap. Whenever I sat down I activated this typewriter - ie. in the bathroom, on the school bus, watching TV - in fact, whenever my mind did not need to be engaged in the outer world.

I typed the same thing over and over – my name and address ending with Southern Hemisphere, Earth, Milky Way, Solar System, Galaxy, Universe. I smile at this now. In Dan Millman's book, "Way of the Peaceful Warrior", many times Socrates asks Dan, *"Where are you?"* One time, Dan ponderously answers in a similar way ending with the Universe. Seems even as a teenager I was unconsciously searching for the answer to the question *"Where am I?"*

I learned to type by letter rather than word. For example, I didn't type the word JULIE, I typed the letters J, U, L, I, E saying each letter in my mind and transferring that to the relevant finger. This way I learned all the keys on the keyboard exceptionally well. I got faster doing this. If I made a mistake I would pretend to backspace and type the correct letter. I practiced every key on this imaginary typewriter. My fingers became an extension of my mind. Ultimately, there was no thinking about it.

Introduction

I won the school prize for typing with 100%. And many years later on a computer I was tested at a recruitment agency and typed 128 words per minute with 100% accuracy. I achieved and surpassed my goal of 90 words per minute. It took 15 years to achieve this goal.

When I left school I applied for a job as a draftsperson at Mount Isa Mines, but was offered a job in the typing pool! Not what I wanted, however, I took the job as a temporary role. You see, I had been accepted into nursing and intended leaving the typing job after 12 months when I turned 18. This was one of those milestone moments where my life changed as a result of this decision to take the job.

The nursing career never eventuated. And here's that "thing" called choice again. I thought 4 years studying to be a nurse was like a prison sentence. I wasn't ready to leave home (it meant moving 1000km away) and I had grown to love my job as a secretary.

It is interesting how one decision, even decisions you think are out of your control, can shape the direction of your life.

It was the practice on my imaginary typewriter for 2 years anywhere, any time that created the foundations of habit which naturally activated when I decided to live a metaphysical life of purpose at 25.

Did I want to do all that practice? No way, but interestingly couldn't go to sleep without doing it!

Sometimes I hated metaphysics and would think to myself *"I don't want anything to do with metaphysics – get out of my life!"* But it wouldn't leave me alone, so I graciously and ungraciously accepted it as part of my world.

I created little rituals. They may have only been 5 minutes, but I still did them. And this practice created the foundations for what I do today.

The Experiment

I experimented with a type of psychic reading by going inside bodies of my friends and family. (I later learned that this is called a medical intuitive reading.) It seemed real to me.

After a couple of years of practice, my father came to visit. When he heard what I had been up to, he asked me to travel through his body. On describing what I saw, he said *"That's exactly how the doctor described my hiatus hernia."*

I didn't know he had a hernia. I also saw a problem behind his right knee which he said happened during WWII. He was stunned I mentioned this as nobody knew about it, not even Mum.

The next night he asked me to travel through again. He was testing me. This time it was different. There was white liquid everywhere. I felt like a fraud! In the morning, Dad asked me again what I saw. I confessed to feeling like a failure and a fraud.

"It was different this time with "white stuff" everywhere."

Dad was stunned, as he had taken his Mucaine (white) medicine before lying down for the scan. This was so exciting to hear and was tangible proof I had discovered how to see inside the human body.

I practiced in earnest after this, asking God for directions. However, I was given one condition – only enter the body of a person who specifically invited me in. I believe because I have honoured this rule, I can still be accurate in my medical intuitive work today.

"The Extraordinary" TV Show

In 1994 and 1996, I appeared on the television show "The Extraordinary" where the producers tested me on film doing medical intuitive readings, telling people in other cities and countries where I believed they had problems in their bodies.

The response from the public was extraordinary. I was totally unprepared for the consequences of media exposure. At that time, Kay Cottee was mentoring me and she said, *"Julie, you must have at least a handful of people you can call from anywhere in the world 24/7, even if it is 3am in their time zone, and say to them – I just need to talk to someone. Or let them know you are having a crap day or whatever, but you certainly need a small number of people you can reach out to."*

Introduction

I didn't have this support when "The Extraordinary" went to air around the world. I felt isolated. Although I had the advice from Kay, I didn't fully grasp the functionality of creating those boundaries and having an inner circle of people who looked out for me.

Many people were nice to me for their own reasons, but ultimately they thought I would tell them something they wanted to know and I confused this with thinking they wanted to be friends with me. It was quite a process and entailed years of learning discernment to grow my authentic inner circle.

I discovered that when you enter into the metaphysical world you need to be discerning about what you say and to whom.

I worked intensively helping people around the world with medical intuitive readings.

BUT there was a price to pay. I didn't understand the importance of boundaries and erroneously believed if someone asked me to help, regardless of how exhausted I was personally, I was obliged to help them. I went from "being of service" to "a being in servitude" and resenting it.

Eventually, I became too ill to continue and illness gave me a valid excuse/reason to say no. It took me a long time to be able to say no without this being my reason.

Prophecy Being Fulfilled

The years of working energetically every day for other people and not looking after myself had taken their toll. Poor boundaries delivered a price.

The prophecy from Br William was being fulfilled. I had already had a diseased gallbladder and diseased womb removed at age 31 and 32. (At this stage of my metaphysical development, I could see the illness, but couldn't heal it.)

In 1999, I lost weight dramatically over 9 months and my whole system shut down. I ended up in hospital with internal hemorrhaging and lumps on my ovaries were diagnosed. After surgery to remove my ovaries, my doctor told me I was very lucky as one of the lumps was a tumour and if left would have turned to ovarian cancer. I was grateful for a second chance at life.

Six weeks later, I was diagnosed with thyroid cancer. At 40 years, I had managed to develop four thyroid diseases – multi-nodular goitre, Hashimoto's (causing underactive thyroid), Plummer's Disease (causing overactive thyroid) and papillary carcinoma (thyroid cancer). I went back to the operating theatre and had my thyroid removed.

Another test was to come; the cancer was attached to my left vocal cord nerve and it was damaged during surgery. I lost my voice for a year which was very embarrassing. A Speech Therapist taught me how to use the breath in my lungs to activate my chest muscles in a way that would make my damaged vocal cord vibrate when I wanted to speak. Amazingly, after a few months of intensive practice, I could speak again. But only if I have air in my lungs. I use this air as my instrument to communicate.

I had a chat with God at this time and promised if I learned to talk again I would step up and share my work with the world. With gratitude, I learned to talk again and now share this work with you.

Why Did You Create So Much Illness In Your Body?

With everything I have learned on my journey, I ask myself this question often. This is a complicated question and one which I hope anyone who suffers from illness asks themselves as well.

You see, as a typical Libran I craved harmony and avoided conflict. Consequently, I suppressed my fear and anger in an attempt to create a peaceful life. And sorrow, well it just wasn't allowed!

I didn't have an opinion except in a safe environment and by internalizing my fear, sorrow and anger, these emotions literally rotted my body from the inside out.

Four throat diseases, and five if you count severe tonsillitis which led to having my tonsils removed at 21, were very in my face. I had to inspect this pattern of avoidance. It was a difficult and painful process.

A major revelation in understanding my illness was my total lack of boundaries with people. I desperately wanted to feel needed. Somehow I had linked feeling needed to being loved.

This lack of boundaries set up a pattern of giving all of my life force away to feed my neediness. It was my form of addiction, and disease was the consequence. I didn't wake up from cancer surgery and understand all of this. In fact, I still had to:

- deal with more surgery to remove an ovarian cyst the size of a grapefruit which was wrapped around my left ureter;
- make the discovery that gluten inflamed my bowel to the extent of causing bowel blockages;
- deal with a growing lump the size of a golf ball in my breast which I handled through my own healing templates, naturopathic remedies and healer friends;
- deal with tumours in my bowel which thankfully have now stopped growing; and
- deal with a relapse of thyroid cancer which is now in remission.

Why didn't you heal yourself?

People say to me, *"Why didn't you heal yourself?"* The daily healing meditations I developed and still use kept me alive, giving me the opportunity to discover my pattern of neediness. Another revelation to come out of this journey has been I was carrying deep soul sorrow.

Self-understanding is a journey not a destination. When you understand what you do that doesn't serve you, interestingly you don't do it anymore.

I have established strong boundaries with inner and outer wellness. Are you ready to transform your inner and outer worlds?

You can do it, too!

Chapter Notes

Chapter 1
How To Cleanse Your Energy

I share this information from the presumption that we have 7 bodies:

1. Physical
2. Emotional
3. Mental
4. Spiritual
5. Auric
6. Energy
7. Etheric

You will most likely be familiar with the first 4 and possibly 5, but may not be familiar with 6 and 7.

- The **physical body** is what you see – it is tangible.

- The **emotional body** resides within the cells of the physical body.
- The **mental body** is your mind or the ego.
- The **spiritual body** relates to your spirit or soul rather than to physical nature or matter – so, it is intangible.
- The **auric body** is a subtle emanation of light around your physical body – this can sometimes be seen with the physical eye, but most often is seen by the third or inner eye.
- The **energy body** is a term for a complex web of interactions of energy centres in your body which correspond to your "chakras".
- The **etheric body** is the vehicle or the instrument of astral energy. It gives vitality, health, life and organisation to your physical body.

Before you can start doing anything metaphysical such as exploring your boundaries, growing your intuition or developing your psychic gifts, you need to know the basics of how to cleanse your energy.

Why do you need to cleanse your energy?

Once you start exploring the hidden worlds of metaphysics, psychic realms, intuition and inter-dimensional travel, you will need to be conscious of you the **"energy being"** that exists within your human form.

By being aware of your subtle bodies you will have the sensitivity to travel beyond your known boundaries and experience multi-dimensional journeys.

Cleansing your energy body of any energy that doesn't belong to your subtle bodies is crucial to moving forward with living an exceptional metaphysical life.

Plus, you need a benchmark of your subtle bodies, so you don't take ownership and responsibility for "stuff" that's not yours. You don't want to bring negative entities/energy into your energy body. You do need to be aware of what we call psychic/energy vampires and make sure your energy is protected.

Now, I don't want to sound alarmist in your first chapter, however, there are a number of things to consider here:

- There are people who unconsciously suck energy from others. These people are often unwell, needy and don't have the ability to light their inner flame *you most probably have experienced this yourself, and know the type of person I am talking about here*;
- There are people who practice black magic/occult to deliberately drain your energy or harm you energetically *this is more difficult to pick up because these people are more cunning and may present to you physically as someone you should or could trust*; and
- There are negative entities that prey on people with weak energetic boundaries who explore metaphysics and the unseen worlds *this can be particularly so for people who explore these worlds through the use of recreational drugs*.

I have personally experienced all of these during my metaphysical journey and the best way of protecting yourself against unseen forces is:

- Become familiar with how your energy body feels so you recognise when something is wrong or out of balance energetically in your bodies;
- Cleanse your energy regularly using one or more of the methods below; and
- Protect your energy (more on this in chapter 2).

You may not have considered cleansing your energy before, so this is going to take discipline to get into the habit of cleansing your energy regularly. I recommend you do this every day – but if you forget, you haven't done any harm, simply do it when you remember and then continue as a daily routine. Once you grasp the concepts and become familiar with them you'll be able to do them easily in a few minutes each day.

I want to share with you a number of ways to personally cleanse you, your home and your work environment.

Personal Cleansing

This is about cleansing your energy body and keeping your energy clear of any connections with people who drain your energy without you being aware of it.

It has been designed to cleanse your energy bodies (auric, energy and etheric) and rejuvenate your soul. It is best to use this template before going to sleep. Your body will regenerate and rejuvenate during sleep and you'll wake up feeling vital, alive and in high spirits.

Template: Personal Cleansing

- Imagine you are walking along a dirt path in the country.
- You are dissociated from the image of you (this means a part of you is watching the rest of you walking along the path).
- As you look closely you will notice that there are threads and ribbons; maybe even young trees or mature trees attached to your body (these are connections made with people throughout the day – and can be represented here as anything that comes to mind).
- Every thought or physical interaction with another person makes a connection to your energy bodies.
- For the deepest rejuvenating and regenerating healing to occur during sleep – it is useful to remove all connections to your energy bodies.
- Remove the threads, ribbons, trees – whatever you see or feel is connected to you.
- Cut them, pull them out, burn them – do what intuitively comes to you.
- Continue walking along the path, you will notice that the image of you is starting to fade – this is good.
- You also notice that the connections are becoming more subtle – remove these subtle connections, too.

How to cleanse your energy

- When you are almost completely faded associate back into the subtle form, lift your eyes and look into the distance, you will see a tunnel filled with golden light.
- Your almost faded body is pulled quickly into the light and this is where you will rest and rejuvenate.
- Your energy body completely dissolves in this golden light.
- You are now resting in the Divine Embrace of the God Source.
- You will be kept safe and protected – your soul will rejuvenate and regenerate and when you wake up you will feel clear, refreshed and vital.

Historically, when people do this meditation before bed, they wake up feeling refreshed from a deep rejuvenating sleep. If you would like a recorded copy of this meditation go to Insight Timer insig.ht/gm_1270.

Exercise: Cleansing Your Home

This following template is one I have used many times, not only for myself, but I've been flown to other cities to do this for clients to clear negative energy and harmonise their homes. You can do this for yourself.

You need a white candle – just the normal candle that we keep in the cupboard for a power blackout is best.

Wrap about 15cm (6in) of alfoil around the bottom of the candle, creating an alfoil cup to catch any dripping wax. Light your candle and walk through your entire house, going into every corner of every room and over the furniture.

With medium speed, raise the candle up to the ceiling and back down again. As you do this, say this mantra:

"I cleanse this room in God's light."

If black smoke comes off the candle repeat the process until no black smoke comes off the candle. The black smoke leaves evidence on the white candle.

I have to be honest and say I was sceptical when I was told about this ritual.

The Art of Self-Healing

I didn't believe in rituals, and I certainly didn't think it would have any impact on the energy of the building.

I was wrong. I experimented with this and was stunned to find some corners had black smoke and others didn't and more so, was incredulous when there was a difference in the energy of the house after I was finished. I also noticed the positive impact on the relationships and behaviour of everyone who lived in the house.

Don't take my word for it. Experiment with this yourself.

Confession time: I did this ritual during the day because I didn't want the neighbours to think I had totally lost it. I'm not aware of a particular time of day that is more potent to do this, so choose a time that feels right for you.

Exercise: Cleansing Your Work Environment

You can use crystals to cleanse your work environment. If you do this, it is important to also cleanse your crystals regularly. This video and article tells you how to cleanse your crystals in a number of different ways.

It has been scientifically proven that having a plant on your desk or close to your work environment will also impact on you in a positive way.

> *"No matter how token, plants are the ambassadors of friendliness; they enable an ambience that is not controlled, robotic, confined – instead by having nature inside, the impression is created of a calm, open, homelike experience.*
>
> *It is not just the aesthetic or psychological impressions that plants make but how plants scientifically put a person at ease that add value to interior plantscaping. Green triggers a response in the sympathetic nervous system to relieve tension in the blood vessels and thus lower the blood pressure, green lowers heart rate and provides an instant feeling of rest and recovery.*
>
> *Dr. Billy C. Wolverton from the John C. Stennis Space Centre recommends for optimum employee health benefit, placing a plant on*

How to cleanse your energy

one's desk, or within six to eight cubic feet of where most of the person's daily activity occurs."

Source: Interior landscaping in the workplace, benefits to business - Fiann Ó Nualláin

In light of this research, if you work in an office, and don't have a plant, I recommend you buy one to put on your desk. Do your own experiment. This is Fiann's list of top 10 plants for the office:

1. Kentia Palm
2. Spathiphyllum spp (peacelily)
3. Chlorophytum spp (spiderplant)
4. Philodendron spp
5. Dracaena spp
6. Ficus spp
7. Scindapsus/Epipremnun
8. Hedra helix (ivy)
9. Syngonium spp
10. Sansevieria spp (snakeplant)

The Art of Self-Healing

Chapter Notes

Chapter 2
How To Protect Your Energy

It's very important to protect your energy and this chapter will show you how to protect your:

- personal energy
- home
- car, and
- loved ones.

When you develop a habit of protecting your energy each day – you experience a shift in your energy throughout the day and certainly by the end of your busy day.

Have you ever hung up the telephone after chatting with a friend or loved one and suddenly felt that you:

- needed a rest, or

- a strong cup of coffee, or
- to go outside into the sunshine, or
- do something to give your energy levels a boost?

What happened? You consciously or unconsciously gave your energy resources to that person.

There are times when this is okay, but you do need to rejuvenate your personal reservoir regularly, or you'll suffer from fatigue and depression, which can impact on your overall health and well-being.

Psychic Vampires

Have you ever thought that some of your friends and loved ones are psychic vampires? That's kind of a harsh thought to have, but you could be right on the money with that thought.

Yes, there are people who have an ability to drain your energy – either consciously or unconsciously – and they are called psychic vampires.

You may not recognise them as they look like "normal" folk.

For example, if someone is in trouble, they tell you their troubles and you sympathise, empathise and look to find solutions for them – you are giving them your energy. Sometimes it is appropriate to do this, but if it becomes a regular occurrence your energy is literally being sucked out of you. This is not a good thing.

The healer / nurturer / like to be needed people suffer from this form of energy attack more than other archetypes.

What often happens is people tell you they feel fantastic when they talk to you and say things like you're such a great listener and friend. This is the seduction of helping people.

YES! They feel great and unfortunately you feel like crap after they leave or even while they are still on the telephone or with you. Does this sound familiar – you override your intuition and convince yourself that you've been a good friend and it's all okay?

If you are going to talk to these people learn to protect your energy.

Personal Protection

Template: Magic Mirror Cylinder

This template works well for protecting your energy from negative thoughts, words and actions.

If you find you are being drained by loved ones, friends, work colleagues, or even complete strangers experiment with this template.

If you can't visualise – then pretend you are doing this. It will still work and protect you from negative, draining situations.

- Imagine you are standing inside a cylinder.
- The outside of the cylinder is completely mirrored.
- The inside of the mirror is warm, comfortable, safe and filled with a beautiful light (you choose what colour you want – each time you use this template).
- You may also smell a beautiful, subtle perfume. You may recognise the scent – it doesn't matter if you don't experience this or recognise it – this is an added dimension to your energy protection.
- Once you feel comfortable in your magic cylinder, say the Prayer of The Cylinder:

    "Only that which is for my highest good may pass through this magic mirror everything else is reflected back to its source in a kind manner."

If you feel like you are being psychically attacked or being drained by energy vampires, use this template daily.

If you want to make your prayer more personal and longer – transform this simple prayer into one that feels right for you.

Template: Tongue To The Roof Of The Mouth

This template was taught to me by a naturopath from Europe who was my lecturer whilst studying naturopathy many years ago. His name was Sid Van Emden.

He gave a lesson on kinesiology and said anyone who was sensitive energetically to other people's energy should learn to do this and consciously use it during vulnerable communication.

Sid tested a number of the students using this method and we were all amazed at the results. This template really strengthens your energy boundaries.

- Behind your top front teeth you will find a ridge.
- Just behind that you will find a spot that sits between the ridges of both sides of your top front teeth.
- Place the tip of your tongue in this "sweet" spot – it will tickle slightly when you have your tongue in the right spot.

Find someone who can do kinesiology. Or go to http://bit.ly/12LQSTj to print the instructions for simple muscle testing. These instructions are shared with permission from gifted Kinesiologist - Dr Andrew Powell and his book "The Money Is In The Mindset".

Either muscle test yourself or get someone to muscle test you while you are thinking about an unpleasant event. It seems to be more dramatic and validating when you have someone else muscle test you.

STEP 1: Think of an unpleasant event, make sure you **DON'T** have the tip of your tongue to the "sweet" spot in the roof of your mouth. Muscle test.

You will find it very difficult to resist the pressure.

STEP 2: Now, think of that unpleasant event again and this time put the tip of your tongue to the "sweet" spot in the roof of your mouth.

You should be able to resist the pressure of the muscle testing.

If you can't resist the test with your tongue in the "sweet" spot, you don't have your tongue in the correct position.

So experiment until you can think of the unpleasant event and resist the pressure of the muscle testing. This way you will know you have located the correct position for your tongue.

This is a priceless treasure when you remember to use it.

Template: Prayer Of Protection

If you feel that your energy is being zapped because you are working or living in a negative or toxic environment, one of the things you can do is activate a simple Prayer of Protection.

Other times I recommend you use this method of protection is when you are doing:

- hands on energy healing
- distance healing
- medical intuition scans
- going into crowded areas, for example:
    - concerts
    - cinemas
    - shopping malls

Also activate it when you are receiving healing or therapies, particularly if you are an empath and sensitive to other people's energy. You would do this in circumstances such as:

- massage
- facial
- reflexology
- distance healing
- hands on healing.

I learned this Prayer of Protection from Rev. Marilyn O'Sullivan in 1987 – and I still use it today:

> *"In the Name of Jesus Christ, I call upon the Spirits of Light to stand guard at the doorway of my Soul and to guide me in the ways of Truth, Love and Light and to protect me from the forces of Darkness and Deception. Amen"*

If this prayer resonates with you, then use it, too. If it doesn't, create one of your own and use it as often as you feel you need to.

I've shared this Prayer with you because it's what I say when I do energy healing, a medical intuitive scan or distance healing and when I go to crowded places or simply don't feel safe energetically.

Template: Energy Protection Egg

Use this template if you are feeling vulnerable or frightened whether this is physically or metaphysically.

The way this template works is to imagine you are standing inside an energy egg and the perimeter of this energy egg is made up of gold crosses.

Repeat this mantra "Please God Protect Me" until you feel safe again. This may be 5 times or 200 times, there is no set number for this.

Have you ever woken with an eerie feeling that you are not alone in your room, or you feel as if your body is paralysed, but you are awake – and sometimes your eyes are open, or it seems you are looking down on your body lying in your bed and you can see the entire room – even though your body feels paralysed.

This has happened to me about 20-30 times and it can be very frightening. I use this template when this happens. It makes me feel safe – and I go back to sleep.

In 2001, I went on a 4 week meditation retreat located high up in the mountains in California. The accommodation I was staying at was a 20 minute walk along a dark, isolated country road from the retreat centre.

For the first two weeks, I was able to get a lift to and from the retreat centre as there were many other people on retreat as well.

In my third week, I finished my evening meal and had a swim in the hot springs and then realised I had to walk home in the dark on my own without a torch. I had forgotten to take it with me.

Wild thoughts were running through my head – particularly as it was an overcast night – there was no moonlight to guide my way.

Nervously setting off, I turned a bend in the road to find there weren't even any street lights for some comfort and guidance. I was worried about mountain lions and the people in the cars driving past me. I wondered, "*Would they stop and drag me into their cars?*" (as I said – wild thoughts).

I started my 20 minute walk terrified and immediately slipped into my mantra "Please God Protect Me" over and over and surrounding myself with an egg of gold crosses.

A very strange thing started to happen as I looked around me, the darkness started to differentiate. I could see the outline of the trees. They had a faint glow of light around them.

I was looking at a panorama of different images in all shades of grey and black. It was one of the most extraordinarily beautiful landscapes I have ever seen.

The further I walked the more exhilarated I felt. I knew I was safe and protected; and I didn't feel isolated or alone anymore. Even though I was walking a lonely country road in the dark of night in a country I wasn't familiar with – I felt safe.

I had to walk home alone many more nights before the retreat ended. So exhilarated by my first experience, I deliberately walked in the dark because I felt so connected to the Divine Source.

Magic out of terror. There is a saying, *"Face your fear head on and it dissolves."* This happened for me in California and I had forgotten this learning until sharing it with you now.

Your Home

Template: Bubble over house

It's a great feeling to know your home is protected energetically. I taught this to Mum over 20 years ago and she does it every night before going to sleep. Since my Dad died in 1999, she feels safe and protected in her home.

STEP 1: Visualise a bubble of white light surrounding the entire property with a force field of protection.

STEP 2: Say this prayer *"Join the bubble with the land to keep intruders out and keep my home safe. Thank you God for keeping my house safe day and night."*

It's simple and effective.

Template: Magic Blinds

STEP 1: Visualise yellow blinds being pulled down over all of the windows and doors in the house. Do each one individually and when you pull the blind down, witness it transform into a force field of bright yellow light.

STEP 2: Collectively ask that the property be kept safe throughout the night and day.

I use one or the other of these templates when we are away from the house, or if I am alone in the house. Experiment with them or come up with your own.

Your Car

Protecting yourself in a motor vehicle is very wise. I started doing this in 1986 when our children were babies.

I've had many close calls in the car, and I 100% believe we remained safe because of this template.

Template: Car protection

- Imagine your car is surrounded by a skirt of old tyres tied together. They are all the way around the middle of the car.
- Then around the tyres visualise a strong band of golden light.
- Visualise a starting point on the car and imagine you have a magic wand.
- Walk around the car with this wand activating the golden light as you walk around the car – be sure that the end point of the light meets the starting point.
- Now, surround each occupant in the car with a bubble of golden light.
- Lastly, say this prayer with your inner voice to complete the process

> *"Please God protect this car and all the occupants from harm – and ensure that we arrive safely at our destination. Amen"*

This particular template came to me as a vision when we were driving in Canberra, Australia's capital city. I had a premonition while driving and saw this vision spontaneously unfold.

Within minutes of this vision, we were on a huge roundabout with traffic going everywhere. The car to our left didn't give way to us.

How we didn't clip the car cutting in front of us and how the car coming behind us missed our rear end, I'm still at a loss to understand.

Thankfully, we made it through the small gap with inches to spare either way. Since that event, I have used this template thousands of times.

On another occasion my friend wanted to visit Hervey Bay, a beautiful tourist destination in Queensland, Australia. It is about 290km north of

The Art of Self-Healing

Brisbane (Queensland's capital) and it is famous for the humpback whales coming to its waters between July and October. Hervey Bay is the nursery for the new whales. It is also the gateway to the world heritage listed Fraser Island. My parents lived there, so we had somewhere to stay for the weekend.

We both had 2 young children aged between 2-6 years. My friend was recovering from a cold, and I was exhausted from a hard week at work. It was 5.30pm and we had a 4 hour drive in the dark ahead of us – not our favourite time to drive.

We put the 4 children in the back seat with two children sharing the middle seat belt. Neither of us were happy with this arrangement nevertheless we did it.

We decided to take my friend's car as it was newer than mine, and agreed that she would drive the first half of the trip and I would drive the second half.

For some reason, I had an uneasy feeling and activated this protection template twice just to be sure I had done it well.

After about 45 minutes driving, I could see my friend was clearly not well and offered to drive. She was very relieved.

We were 3 hours into our trip and had just come over a mountain between Gympie and Maryborough – the Gunalda Range. There was a passing lane and normally I would scoot around the slower cars and be gone. This particular night I said to my friend, *"I think I'll just sit behind these cars. I feel safe here."*

I was driving at 90km/hour in a 100km zone.

I don't like driving at night because I am fascinated by the headlights coming towards me. A bit like a rabbit caught in the headlights.

I transitioned from the two lanes to one as a number of cars came towards us. Suddenly, I saw something black flick past my vision. It broke my trance and shocked me fully awake.

I pulled the car over to the side of the road. It was a dark night with no moon so it was difficult to see anything.

I worriedly said to my friend, *"I didn't hit that car did I?"* She said, *"No!"*

We got out and ran our hands around the entire car. Everything was still there.

However, I could smell something hot and poked my head back inside the car to check the temperature gauge – it was normal. I checked all the tyres by feeling from the road to the rim of the wheel. They were all okay.

Very shaken from this experience, we got back in the car and kept driving. Much slower now as the car was pulling to the left. I drove about 60-70km/hour.

It was a long 90km drive to my parent's home. We finally made it safely, albeit very exhausted.

Dad came out to welcome us. We were standing beside the car on the driveway chatting and could hear a metallic scraping noise.

We looked down in horror. There was no rubber on the front right hand tyre. There was only a shiny chain mesh surrounding the tyre tube.

I said to Dad, *"My prayers do work! Do you believe me now?"*

In the morning, Dad changed the tyre and we took it down to the tyre shop. When we told them I had driven 90km with 4 kids and 2 adults on that tyre they didn't believe us. In fact, they said it isn't possible! They hung the tyre on their showroom wall like a prize.

The truth is it was a re-tread tyre and the re-tread had come away. That's what I had seen flick past my vision in the brightness of the oncoming traffic headlights. We used to buy re-treads for our cars as well, but never again after that experience.

On our way home in daylight a couple of days later, we came to the place on the highway where it happened. Phew! We noticed there was a 4 metre drop at the side of the road. We could have ended up in that gully and even worse, could all have been killed.

We were looked after that night. I like to believe that my protection template helped us with a tyre miracle.

Do you ever get a strong feeling that something is not going to go right?

We were going on a holiday to Stanthorpe and had to go from Brisbane up through the Great Dividing Range at Cunningham's Gap to get there. The Gap is about 90km west of Brisbane. It is an impressive escarpment of mountains and quite a climb up to the Darling Downs from the coastal region.

I had such a bad feeling about the trip I took out travel insurance for our 3 day holiday to the country. And, yes, I did this particular template several times in the first hour of our journey. In fact, I had just finished doing it before we began climbing The Gap.

This highway is one of the major transport routes for semi-trailers in Australia. They transport our food supply and all manner of product into and out of Queensland on this road. It is common to see 10 semi-trailers one behind the other moving the country's essential supplies from A to B.

Mostly it has one lane down and two lanes up the range. We were travelling on the inside lane beside a car on the outside lane. We came around a bend and there was a semi-trailer overtaking a car and caravan. The semi-trailer was in our lane.

If I had been driving I would have braked and the semi-trailer would have run over the top of us. Thankfully, Frank accelerated fast and somehow squeezed through the gap between the semi-trailer and the car on our left.

After this near miss, I could literally breathe more easily and was flooded with confidence we would be safe for the rest of our holiday.

A Loved One

Do you ever get a sense of disaster or calamity about a loved one?

As a mother, I experienced this many times with our children. And more particularly, after our son turned 18 and started going out to the night clubs on a Friday or Saturday night.

My biggest fear was that he would get into a fight and be bashed, knifed,

How to protect your energy

king hit or worst case scenario killed.

No, I didn't stay up at night waiting for him to come home.

However, sometimes I would wake suddenly from a deep sleep and wonder "*Why am I awake?*", as generally once I'm asleep, I sleep through till morning. So, if I woke up with clarity like this, I would check in on our children's energy field.

99% of the time it was our son and invariably I felt he was in danger. So while still connected energetically to him, I immediately visualised a pillar of golden light descend from the heavens and surround him. You could possibly describe it as angelic in appearance.

Within 15-20 minutes of me doing this he would arrive home safely. And, physical conflict was avoided.

In the morning, when I asked him if there were any problems the night before, there always had been. He'd tell me how dramatically things changed and how he had a strong urge to come straight home.

Template: A loved one protection

I recommend this process if you have a premonition or feel that a loved one needs help.

STEP 1: Connect into the energy of your loved one.

STEP 2: Visualise a pillar of golden light descending from high above come down over your loved one and see them encased in this golden light.

STEP 3: Ask that they be protected from harm and arrive home safely – whether that be to your place or their place, depending on where they live.

The Art of Self-Healing

Chapter Notes

Chapter 3
How To Rejuvenate Your Energy

This chapter is about **rejuvenating** your physical and energy bodies.

It's important you learn how to rejuvenate your energy levels regularly. In my experience, if you don't do this you get a build-up of stress, suffer from fatigue, and your health deteriorates.

What Do I Mean By Rejuvenation?

Rejuvenation in the context of this chapter is where you refill your inner reservoir. This gives you resources to cope with life's ups and downs.

It means taking time for you!

And for the "givers" reading this – YES, that means you have to receive, too.

It can be as simple as receiving a compliment and as huge as going on a retreat and stepping out of the world for a time.

Ways To Rejuvenate

1. *Exercise: Technology Free Time*

Being plugged in 24/7 doesn't give you any downtime. The reality is you are always available and constantly on high alert. The fight or flight mechanism is being abused by being so accessible night and day.

The Art of Self-Healing

The world doesn't fall apart if you go off "the technology grid". In fact, when you plug back in you may find your cyber community is more connected with you because they've missed you.

In the beginning, you miss the adrenalin that comes from the immediacy of this form of communication, but after a while you find you don't miss it at all. Being uncontactable on the cyber grid means you can be fully present in whatever activity or relationship you are engaged in physically.

I have done this for an extended period twice now. One time I went on holidays for three weeks and we turned our mobile phones off for the entire time. The freedom this creates is indescribable.

Being off the grid reminded me of my childhood days when we didn't have television. I reflect with much appreciation that in Mount Isa we didn't get television till about 1971. I was 11.

Can you imagine the freedom we had growing up playing outside? We used our imaginations every day and created our own fantasy worlds. We were *never* bored! We roamed the hills and countryside, always taking food and water as we never knew how long we would be gone. Often it was from sun up to sun down. Sometimes we played under the house building cities in the dirt and being completely absorbed in the moment, just us and nature. There were no distractions from being fully present in life.

A few years ago, we travelled around Tasmania for two weeks and there was little to no mobile phone coverage with our phone plan. We had to contact the outside world the old fashioned way - via a telephone box. Both of these extended periods of being off the technology grid strengthened my relationship with my husband and with our friends.

You don't have to go as far as turning your phone off for an extended period of time, but it would really serve you to have 1 day per week where you put your phone on silent and don't turn your computer on. Consider doing these:

- reconnect with your friends and family
- have a bbq in the park

- play board games – this can be lots of fun
- read a book
- go for a drive in the country
- go for a bush walk
- garden.

Do whatever connects you back into the Divine Stream in a way that works for you. The benefit of this is you experience spontaneous joy. Yes, unexpected and delicious! I highly recommend it.

If you opt-out of the "technology grid" for 1 day per week – you will feel like you have had a holiday. The impact on your ability to rejuvenate your energy levels will be so great you will want to do it more often. If you can't opt-out 1 day per week, it is crucial for your long term well-being to opt-out 1 day per month.

2. Exercise: Patterned Healing Water

In 1994, I went to Taiwan for a holiday and while there I was introduced to a man called "The Admiral". He was an exceptional healer and Qi Gong Master. He was very generous with his time and shared profound wisdom with me. One of the things he demonstrated was the gift of patterning water.

He filled two clean glasses with tap water. I tasted the water in both glasses and they both tasted the same. He put one glass to the side, held the other glass in one hand and placed the other hand over the top of the glass. He closed his eyes and incanted 20 Buddha's names in a particular order. (My understanding is that the Buddhist faith has Buddha's similar to the saints in the Catholic Church.)

When he had finished he asked me to taste the water again. I was amazed to find it tasted like Chinese herbs. Yet the water was still clear and I knew he hadn't added any powder or liquid to it. I felt immediately revitalised as if I had been given a potent tonic to drink.

I didn't learn the order of the Buddha's names, but when I returned home to Australia, I wondered whether it was possible for me to pattern water like "The Admiral" for my clients.

I had a client who had inoperable lung cancer and he was suffering badly from the effects of chemotherapy. He was in great pain and the nausea and the vomiting were debilitating.

So we did an experiment.

I sat quietly holding a glass of water straight from the tap. I imagined being in a room in another dimension. It was an herbalist's cottage from ancient times. The walls were lined from floor to ceiling with shelves containing herbs in packets – some were powdered, others were the whole dried herb. In the centre of the room was a timber table. It was a rustic room – no paint anywhere – just worn timber.

The glass of water was sitting on the timber table. As I scanned the room some of the packets of herbs glowed. I took these packets of herbs out of the shelves and placed them on the table. Each packet was opened and some of the herb placed in the glass of water. The amount ranged from a sprinkle to a pinch to a teaspoon. When all the herbs were in the glass of water, I looked around the room and noticed a basket full of freshly cut flower heads, no stems. I picked a flower from the basket and placed it on top of the glass of water.

Immediately there was an alchemical explosion of bright light and I was transported back into my physical kitchen holding the glass of water. I tasted the water from the glass I was holding and from the second glass that had been set aside. They tasted different.

Amazingly, I had discovered it is possible to pattern water with the vibration of healing herbs. The man with the lung cancer found that by drinking this patterned water his pain and nausea stopped completely. He didn't require any further pain medication and he stopped vomiting.

I can't promise this will happen for you, but it is worth experimenting with this, don't you think? If you find this doesn't work for you right now, keep experimenting as you continue to develop your intuition.

3. Meditation

Meditation is a great discipline to have. If you are not doing so already start the habit of meditating regularly. Seasoned meditators will meditate for an hour or more per day. However, if you are just starting out this may be too much for you.

I recommend beginners start meditating for 5 minutes each day.

Here are some simple 5 minute meditations you can do to help rejuvenate and refill your inner reservoir. As you become accustomed to the process you can increase the length of time you meditate. Although, don't turn it into just another task to do, as you will lose the magic of the process.

For these simple meditations, you can be sitting or lying down. You can sit on a chair, a meditation cushion or stool – wherever you are comfortable. As you develop your meditation style, you may want to sit in a particular posture. But for now the most important thing is to be comfortable and make it easy to develop the daily habit.

Exercise: Breath meditation

- Simply focus on your breath in and your breath out.
- Observe how your nostrils feel as the air is drawn gently through your nose and down the back of your throat into your lungs. As your breath gently flows out of your lungs, up the back of your throat and out through your nose become aware of the hairs on your top lip. What happens when you breathe out?
- Repeat for 5 minutes.

Exercise: Candle meditation

- Instead of focusing on your breath, focus your attention on a candle flame. For this meditation you need to be sitting and remain open-eyed. However, if your eyes spontaneously close, don't force them to remain open.

- If your mind wanders – that's fine – bring it back to the candle when you observe it has become distracted. Once again, focus on the flame.
- Start doing this meditation for 5 minutes and increase the time as you feel moved to.

Exercise: Train Light

- Imagine you are standing at the entrance of a train tunnel and you slowly walk towards a stationary train at the other end of the tunnel.
- The simplicity of this meditation is in the darkness of the tunnel and the circle of bright light drawing you towards it with every step. It is an amazing meditation.

This is the first mediation I learned. I meditated for 15 minutes most days. At the end of the day, my husband could tell the minute he walked through the door whether I had done my 15 minutes meditation. If I hadn't, he would take the children for a walk while I meditated. It made that much difference to the harmony of our home.

Exercise: Sharing Nature's Energy

This template works particularly well if you have been in a negative environment and need to re-energise. When you sit in front of the computer for long periods of time this template helps, too.

You can quickly and easily re-energise yourself with this simple energy exchange.

- Find a tree, plant or grass that appears to be more vibrant and vital than the rest.
- If you are indoors, look out a window or use an indoor plant in your workplace or home.

How to rejuvenate your energy

- If you are outdoors, you have plenty of variety to choose from.
- To activate this template ask the tree or grass or indoor plant if you can share its energy.
- Imagine you can see the energy field around the plant. You may even be able to see the energy field with your eyes open. Tap into this field and use it to refill your depleted energy resources.
- Just as we have an energy field around our body, plants have this energy field around them and you can blend with it.
- As you take a deep breath in, imagine the shape of the infinity symbol dancing between you by visualising the light around the plant being drawn into your lungs with love.
- As you breathe out send this energy back to the plant with gratitude, completing the infinity symbol.
- Repeat this cycle for 3 minutes and feel your energy increase with each breath.
- Enjoy the experience of this much needed tonic.

Use a prayer like this one to activate energy sharing with your chosen tree, grass or indoor plant.

> *"Magnificent tree (/grass/plant) may I share your glorious vitality so that I can replenish my depleted energy reserves. (Breathe it in deeply when you breathe out say) And I send it back to you with my deepest gratitude for your generosity."*

4. Holiday

Take a regular holiday.

It takes two weeks to wind down from your working life and in weeks 3-4 you really rejuvenate and regenerate.

However, if it is not possible to take a long holiday such as a four week holiday, it would benefit you greatly to take one week off every three months.

If that's not possible, dedicate one weekend a month to holiday mode. This doesn't mean you have to go away, but do something special and out of your ordinary routine.

It might be that you pull the phone out of the wall, turn your mobile phone and computer off and not be contactable.

- Hire a bunch of DVDs.
- Buy/borrow a book you've always wanted to read.
- Possibly stay in bed all day.
- Fill the refrigerator with yummy food, so you don't have to go out.

Make it a special weekend. It will improve your mood and how you feel about your life and if you are in a relationship it will improve your relationship, too.

It is even better if you can get away from your home for the weekend. It can be in a tent in a national park or in 5 star luxury. The fun part is that you can choose what you will do:

Have a holiday weekend:

- at home
- in a tent
- in 5 star luxury.

If you have children get them involved in their regular holiday weekend / or day if a whole weekend is not possible.

It is vital to your health and wellbeing to take regular down time and enjoy your life.

I recently read a book written by Ramtha and he says, *"Your life purpose is to experience joy."* How simple is that?

How to rejuvenate your energy

I'm going to add to this and say, your life purpose is to experience joy and wonder! And to do this yes you have to wind down and notice it.

This chapter is about some of the things you can do to rejuvenate and regenerate. Experiment with the above and be creative to come up with other ways you can rejuvenate and regenerate.

Chapter Notes

Chapter 4
Creative and Spontaneous Visualisation

Now we're starting to get into some fun stuff.

Did you know there are two types of visualisation? They are creative and spontaneous visualisation.

What is Spontaneous Visualisation?

*"**Spontaneous visualisation**"* is the type of visualisation that occurs during meditation or when you ponder (ie., think about) a question and a vision pops into your mind randomly. You don't need to DO something to make it happen like when you access your memory and you have to consciously bring that memory into your mind to recall what happened.

With spontaneous visualisation, it just arrives in your mind's eye in a similar way to when you watch a movie for the first time and you don't know what comes next.

Exercise: Spontaneous Visualisation

- Close your eyes for a moment and imagine you are inside a shell. You have not experienced this before, so whatever comes up for you is spontaneous. You are not accessing a memory for the vision to manifest. This is spontaneous visualisation.

What is Creative Visualisation?

"Creative visualisation" is the type of visualisation that occurs when you consciously or actively manipulate, change or deliberately invent what you see in your vision during meditation or when you ponder something. With creative visualisation you transform your vision like an artist changes or enhances a painting.

Exercise: Creative Visualisation

- Go back into the shell you spontaneously visualised in the previous exercise and deliberately put a bench in the centre of the shell and sit on it.
- As you sit there, ask your guide to come into your visualisation. This element is creative visualisation. When the guide arrives, this could be spontaneous as you may not have seen this guide before. If you know what your guide looks like, you can manifest them in this vision and that would be **creative** visualisation.

What is the significance of using both types of visualisation?

Before we move on with this chapter, let me help you if you think you can't visualise?

If you suck at visualisation, experiment with me. Over the years, I have found 25% of people say they can't visualise. In fact, 24% can – they just don't realise they are visualising. The other 1% have a medical condition which prevents them from visualising, but they can feel. Feeling is the next best way to communicate with your body.

If you are one of the 24% – this is for you – if you aren't skip to the next section.

Exercise: Access Memory

- Sit in your lounge room. Now describe your bedroom. Write down all the things you can recall about your room. For example, you have a chest of drawers, a walk-in robe, an ensuite, a feather doona, glass doors onto a balcony and a pot plant in the right hand corner of the room.

If you don't look through the door of your bedroom, how can you write down so many details about your room?

Well the answer is you remember what it looks like. You access the memory faculty of your mind and you either just know, or you literally see a vision of your room and you are able to recall it similar to when you watch a movie. This is the same faculty you need to use for creative and spontaneous visualisation.

With spontaneous visualisation you won't have a memory you can access. It just runs like a "new movie" in this faculty. With creative visualisation you can either change a memory or alter the "new movie".

For example, let's go back to your bedroom; you could change the doona cover to be black and red (something that you've never seen before). You can creatively change your bedroom in this dimension. The creative aspect is when you decide you will change the doona cover and the spontaneous aspect is when the cover pops into your vision and it is something you've never seen before.

I hope this makes sense.

The power of visualisation

Over time, I've discovered the body responds to images rather than words. So, if you want your body to transform or change – you need to show your body what you want it to do, rather than using words. The best way to do this is through visualisation.

The voice you hear in your head will not help change the energy in your body. However, the images or visions you see in your mind's eye can most definitely change the way your body feels.

Below is a quote taken from the book, *Love's Executioner* by Irvin D Yalom. When I found this revelation, it unlocked the reason visualisation is so powerful for human beings.

> "... the mind thinks in images but, to communicate with another, must transform image into thought and then thought into language. That march, from image to thought to language, is treacherous. Casualties occur: the rich, fleecy texture of image, its extraordinary plasticity and flexibility its private nostalgic emotional hues – all are lost when image is crammed into language.
>
> Great artists attempt to communicate image directly through suggestion, through metaphor, through linguistic feats intended to evoke some similar image in the reader. But ultimately they realise the inadequacy of their tools for the task...
>
> ... a third barrier to the full knowing of another lies not in the one who shares but in the other, the knower, who must reverse the sharer's sequence and translate language, back to thought, back to image – the script the mind can read. It is wildly improbable that the receiver's image will match the sender's original mental image."

It isn't any wonder we have such difficulty with communicating when most of the people in the world are not conscious of the true nature of our internal language system. Perhaps the Egyptians had it right with hieroglyphics depicting their stories.

When do you use visualisation?

I recommend you use visualisation every day and develop your gift of telepathy as an added resource to aiding better communication. Telepathy communicates via images because it is mind to mind communication.

"You may say I'm a dreamer" – a line from the song "Imagine" by John Lennon. This is a good thing to be – "a dreamer". Dreaming is food for your soul. It transforms your physical, mental, emotional and spiritual bodies.

Day-dreaming is another word for visualisation.

If you spend at least 15 minutes each day doing visualisation – both spontaneously and creatively – you feel happier and more joyful, and you can manage life's challenges more decisively and with less stress.

Is 15 minutes of daydreaming the ideal – NO – 30-60 minutes is ideal, but if you are time poor, or working up to nurturing yourself – 5-15 minutes is a good place to start.

Healing Templates

Since 1984, I've discovered hundreds of healing templates. I've taught them to my clients and have repeated some of them over and over with great results.

In the first instance, each template was purely spontaneous. Then I wondered if I repeated the process with another client, would I get a similar result. This repeated use turns spontaneous visualisation into creative visualisation, with you as the director of your movie.

This is my favourite part of metaphysics and it may well become yours, too.

You will find some of these healing templates in Chapter 12.

Chapter Notes

Chapter 5
Your Metaphysical Body Language Helps You Heal Yourself

Through unravelling the great wisdom of interpreting my metaphysical body language to heal myself, I have found that others can use it to heal themselves, too.

Iridologists say the eyes tell an amazing story. Apparently my eyes tell a story of a weak constitution. This means the building blocks of good overall health are not strong in my body. However, I have turned this weakness into my greatest strength – medical intuition.

One of the ways I've developed this medical intuition is to unpack what I call our metaphysical body language.

Just as one learns to read, count, climb, or acquire any new skill, I have learned to read the stories of the body. These stories help me follow the treasure hunt for subtle nuances and clues the body so graciously provides regarding the impact of feelings, thoughts and actions on our being.

It may surprise you to learn clues are given every moment of every day about where the blockages are in the body/mind. Once you start to recognize the signs you have the opportunity to make changes early, thus avoiding health problems down the track.

In this chapter, I share with you the bones of what I have discovered. And it is my hope; you will use what I share as a guide to discover your own metaphysical body language. I feel learning to read your own body and embarking on an inner pilgrimage of self-discovery and self-understanding is the greatest and most empowering adventure you can take. So let's get started.

Note: The metaphysical body language I share with you here is a basic guide to self-understanding and locating the thoughts and actions you make which trigger energy blockages in your body. It is not everything you need to know about healing yourself, but it is a great start.

Also, it is important you understand you are responsible for your health and well-being. If you are experiencing a problem with your health see your health care provider as well as doing the inner work.

Left and Right Sides of the body

An interesting phenomenon I witnessed whilst unpacking this metaphysical body language was how the left and right side of the body tell its own unique story.

When someone has a blockage (pain or disease) in the left side of their body, the root cause of the problem is from an emotional situation more than 2 years prior. When someone has a blockage in the right side of their body, the source is from an emotional situation somewhere from the present day back 2 years.

My conclusion is that the left side of the body represents emotional blockages from the past (more than 2 years ago) and the right side of the body represents emotional blockages from the present (in the last 2 years). However,

Your metaphysical body language

if the symptoms present as follows: *"What if I have had this pain for 10 years and it is on the right side?"* When this is the case, I review what has compounded this problem in the past 2 years.

Below are the common messages I have learned from observing the metaphysical body language of myself and clients over the past 30 years.

Arms | Hands

The arms and hands represent RECEIVING and invariably people who have a problem with this part of their body, struggle with receiving. They are genuinely nice, giving, caring people who would give you the shirt off their back if you needed it. However, when someone offers these people the shirt off their back (metaphorically speaking), this archetype generally says, "No thank you, I'm fine!" Or they find someone else to pass it forward to.

If you experience arm or hand problems practice receiving with gratitude. It may feel unfamiliar to you and you will resist doing it. This is why I suggest you PRACTICE, PRACTICE and more PRACTICE. You will break down your super neural highway of non-receiving and this can take some time if you do it on your own. Alternatively, you can find someone who specializes in this type of work to re-pattern your subconscious to receiving mode.

Underlying the pattern of not receiving with ease and grace are a plethora of limiting beliefs and it is those beliefs that need to be addressed either on your own, or with a practitioner skilled in this work.

My personal and professional experience suggests it is much quicker, easier, and more productive to work with a practitioner to release these limiting beliefs.

Exercise: Receive

- When you are offered help, an item, a compliment, support with no strings – **RECEIVE** it gracefully. The secret is to receive **without** feeling any obligation to repay or give back to the person offering it.
- You can "pay it forward" as this movement keeps the energy of giving

and receiving moving. Remember, you cannot give what you do not have! Be sure to fill your inner reservoir first before giving.

Hip | Leg | Knee | Ankle | Toes

The hip to toe part of the body represents where you are on your life path and it falls into 3 primary areas career, relationship and home. Yes, there are other areas of your life that will impact your hip to toe physiology, but if you consider these 3 you will most likely locate what's really going on from an emotional perspective.

Health and wellness is largely about the impact of your emotions on your body and when you understand how this happens it will help you unravel this patterning and shift those blocks.

Hips:

If you have a problem with your HIP this indicates you are consciously or unconsciously considering a change in career, home or relationship. It is the beginning phase of the journey, and can raise some powerful resistance or trigger your limiting beliefs around your decision.

For example, beliefs such as these:

- am I good enough
- do I deserve a new house, new job, new partner
- am I worthy
- what if I don't like it? Often the fear of not liking what you desire is the biggest hurdle to overcome. Have you ever heard the saying *"better the devil you know than the devil you don't know"* – this fits right in here with this limiting belief.

Good news! The further down the leg you go the further along the path you are to achieving your dream, goal, shift.

Knee:

The hips, knees, ankles and toes are all moving elements of the stepping forward action and when there is a physical problem in these areas, this is your signal to inspect what is keeping you out of flow with your life.

> **Personal Story:** *I injured my left knee at a time when I was making changes in my career and home. I tore the meniscus and have cartilage damage. This injury is managed well most of the time and when it flares up I struggle to walk without pain. Funnily enough, the pain occurs when I have made a decision out of alignment with my true path.*
>
> *To remedy a flare up, I have to objectively inspect my thoughts, decisions, and actions just prior to my knee becoming painful or locking up. I endeavor to reverse the decision, change my thoughts and often need to seek practitioner assistance. Generally, going to a practitioner is necessary when I am unable to locate the decision or thought which triggered the flare up. Low and behold, the answer invariably weaves itself into my awareness, or pops into my consciousness while I am receiving treatment.*

Feet:

When it comes to feet I consider this question *"Are you standing firm in your position on this issue?"* For example, if you sprain your ankle, this is an indication that you are not confident of your decision. It may be that you need more information, or you have a limiting belief around deserving.

Toes:

The toes indicate you are now at the stage of crossing your "t"s and dotting your "i"s. Really inspect the finer details of your decision before launching forward as there is potentially something not quite right for this block to manifest.

I get excited when I see people with toe problems because I know they are

The Art of Self-Healing

standing on the cliff edge and ready to launch into their new world. This tells me there is one more blockage to overcome.

The same goes for me – when I kick my toe (as painful as it can be) I rejoice in the experience. For I know I'm about to have a huge breakthrough. Weird, I know! But true nevertheless. Yes, I even rejoiced when I broke my toe recently.

Exercise: Release Pain

- Review the decisions you have made recently. Are they in-line with your purpose? Do you feel in flow with these decisions? If no, where is the conflict? Change this part of your decision. Sometimes it only needs a tweak.

- Once you have identified the problem, put your best (the one that feels most comfortable) hand on the affected part of your body and say out loud, *"I don't have to do that anymore!"* Repeat these words out loud until you really believe them. Energy will rush through your torso when your body believes you mean it.

- If the pain doesn't completely leave your body, ask yourself what is it you are not doing for your purpose and need to be and say out loud, *"I can do that!"* Repeat these words out loud until you really believe them. Again, energy will rush through your torso when your body believes you mean it.

- Has the pain gone? If not, look deeper within to locate the precise action or thought triggering the pain.

- This technique works best on new pain problems. And you must honor the commitment you make with these words, otherwise the pain will return because you haven't made the changes permanently.

Lower Back

Generally, lower back is about tension around finances. Questions to consider if lower back is a problem for you are:

- Am I behaving responsibly with my finances?
- What am I afraid will happen?
- What am I doing to increase my financial security and do I believe it is possible?
- Am I taking responsibility for other people's financial wellbeing?
- Do I have a savings plan?
- Do I have a budget?

Your answers to these questions will help you locate the emotional blockage causing the pain in the lower back.

Again, if it is on the left side look to the past and if it is the right side look to the present for the emotional block.

If it is the spine specifically look at the structure of how you manage your finances as the spine is about the structure of your life. There is more on this in the spine section.

Exercise: Pay Me First

- If you haven't already, start a "Pay Me First" account and put 10% of what you earn into this account before you pay anyone else and watch it grow. As your money grows you will gain a sense of financial security and ease the tension in your lower back. If per chance, 10% is out of your depth, begin with 5%, 2% or 1%. The important thing here is to start!

Breasts

The breasts are about nurturing. When a baby is born, traditionally, the breasts are the food supply. The intimate connection between mother and baby has long been used as a symbol of nurturing.

So, when problems happen with the breasts this generally shows there is a pattern of non-nurturing in one or more areas of your life.

How many times have you heard people say *"Why did it happen to her, she is such a nice, giving, caring, supportive person. And then there are people like xxx who don't care about other people, take, take, take and think only of themselves – why don't they get cancer or something?"*

Let's consider the above scenario, although the person with breast cancer is a nice person, giving, caring, supportive and the first one in to help out, the question is do they give to, care for and support themselves with as much energy and enthusiasm. Or do they come second to others. My experience in observing this giving personality archetype is they empty their inner reservoir of energy and vitality by giving it away willy nilly – and don't completely refill it for one reason or another. So in keeping with the reservoir metaphor the water line goes lower and lower until there is nothing left in the tank for when they need it.

This doesn't mean you stop giving and being caring. There has to be balance. There needs to be as much inflow as outflow. The reservoir needs to be full and there must be self-nurturing.

It is not selfish to self-nurture or receive nurturing from others. It is ESSENTIAL for your health and wellbeing. Once again, remember you cannot give what you do not have! Be sure to fill your inner reservoir first.

Exercise: Retreat Day

- Every 4-6 weeks, stay in bed all day on your own for 1 day. Sleep in, read a book, listen to music, unplug from the grid – no phone, no iPad, no computer, stock up on healthy treats, drink tea, meditate.
- Re-fill your inner reservoir in whatever way works for you. I know this works – I have been doing it since my cancer diagnosis in 2000. It has been instrumental in my amazing and phenomenal healing.

Abdomen – Womb | Ovaries | Bowel

The abdomen contains three central areas - the bowel, the ovaries and the womb.

Womb

The womb is where conception happens. This is where new life is born. When there is a problem in the womb generally speaking, there are limiting beliefs around giving birth to new ideas and a fear of deserving and being worthy of the magnificence you desire.

Ovaries | Testicles

The ovaries and testicles are the point of creation, the very beginning. When there are problems with the ovaries and testicles there is generally resistance to change yet at the same time strong desire for change. This sets up internal conflict and incongruence.

Bowel

We have the small intestine (bowel) and the large intestine (bowel).

The small intestine supports us nutritionally and the large bowel removes the waste. It depends on where the problem is in the bowel as to what message you are being given.

A problem in the small bowel is a sign your soul is not receiving the nutrition it needs – this could be because you are literally not feeding your soul, or you can't absorb or understand what you are feeding it.

A problem in the large bowel is a sign of holding on (in the case of constipation) and with diarrhea which can be swift and sudden indicates not absorbing all the information needed.

Exercise: Bowel Healing Elixir

- A great healing elixir for the bowel is to imagine a royal blue ball of light (about the size of a golf ball), put it into your mouth and swallow it.
- Imagine you are made of glass and watch the ball of light slide down your oesophagus, whiz around your stomach, down into the

duodenum, into the small intestine (looks like a bunch of hairpin bends in a road), up the large intestine on the right, over the top of the abdomen and down the left side, through the colon and out the anus.

Do this from the perspective of being associated with your body. What this means is you are observing the blue ball of light from inside your body, not witnessing it in your holographic body in your screen of mind.

The secret to getting the best out of this exercise is when an outside thought comes (ie., other than travelling from mouth to anus) go back to the beginning and start again. With practice this exercise will help you have control of the tension in your bowel. I use it to manage IBS spasms. It also helps you have control over peristalsis which helps with reducing constipation.

Ears

The ears are one of the traditional 5 senses – and they are the means by which we hear. When there are problems with the ears this indicates not wanting to hear or being blocked from hearing something of importance.

Everyone can experience the download of information or understand what their resistance is to discovering an answer. Whether you hear with your physical ears or not does not change this process. Therefore, people who are deaf or hearing impaired are also able to participate and examine the symbolism and contemplate the question – *"What is it I am not hearing?"*

Exercise: Magnify Hearing

- Sit quietly in nature. Locate and isolate the individual sounds closest to you – listen for 2 minutes, become really familiar with them.
- Move your hearing focus out to about 50 meters (we'll call this the middle distance) and locate and isolate the sounds at this distance for 2 minutes.
- Leave these sounds and move your hearing focus out to about 200 meters, locate and isolate the sounds coming from this far away for

2 minutes.
- Now open your awareness to all of the sounds simultaneously.

This exercise will enhance your inner and outer hearing faculties.

Eyes

The eyes are our seeing faculty. When there is a problem with the eyes, this indicates a blockage with seeing all that is available. Our internal filters can hide vital information from us. Eyes that experience difficulty are a signal for you to look deeper into what you are not seeing.

This is also significant when your inner sight appears to be blocked. Look at the underlying emotions and you will locate where you need to spend some time.

People who are blind or vision impaired can participate and examine this symbolism and contemplate the question – *"What is it I am not seeing?"*

Exercise: Eye Balm

- Sit in a peaceful, quiet place.
- Close your eyes and place the palms of your hands over your eyes.
- Imagine coming from your palms a beautiful, soothing, healing light penetrating into the depths of your eyes and going deeper into your inner third eye.
- Feel your eyes being bathed in this light for 5 minutes.

Teeth

We use our teeth to bite and chew. Sometimes we can feel we have bitten off more than we can chew. When there are problems with the teeth – look at how you manage the things you take on in your life.

If teeth problems show up unexpectedly review what you've been doing and you may find you've bitten off more than you are comfortable with. Focus on smaller elements of the bigger picture. This next exercise is a condensed version sourced from www.naturalnews.com..

Exercise: Oil Pulling

- On an empty stomach (best done first thing in the morning), put a dessertspoon of organic cold-pressed oil (coconut, olive, sesame or sunflower) into your mouth and swish and pull it through your teeth for 15-20 minutes.
- <u>Do not</u> swallow the oil. Spit it out (in the bin or outside). Brush your teeth with toothbrush #1 (no toothpaste).
- Rinse your mouth with salty water (use Himalayan rock or Celtic sea salt).
- Pull the salty water through your teeth.
- Brush your teeth with toothbrush #2 with natural toothpaste. This is an ongoing life choice.

Neck

We use our neck to turn from side to side and see all opportunities on our path. When a problem with the neck shows up, this tells me a decision is about to be made and all the opportunities have not been considered.

Tension builds up as intuition suggests something important is missing. The left side of the neck indicates an opportunity with links to the past (more than 2 years back) and the right side of the neck indicates an opportunity with links from now back over the past 2 years.

Exercise: Release Neck Tension

- Place your chin on your chest and gently look left keeping your chin as close to your chest as possible and then look gently to your right.
- Slowly look to the left and right several times – keeping your chin as close as possible to your chest. Not only will you keep your neck

more subtle, but you will also exercise the muscles going down under your shoulder blades. If this causes pain, don't do it and see a practitioner of your choice. However, do consider opening up to further opportunities before making whatever decision is happening in your world right now.

- You can use the same technique as Exercise #9 too, page 58. Wrap your hands around your neck and consider opening up to seeing all your opportunities and say, "*I can do that!*" until your body believes you.

- If you are still in pain, consider what you are doing to block new opportunities from your path, put your hands on either side of your neck and say, "*I don't have to do that anymore!*" until your body believes you.

Spine

The spine provides the structure for the body. When the spine has problems, the place to inspect is the structure of your life. You may feel unsupported in certain areas of your life such as your career, relationships, personal development or spiritually.

Exercise: Spine Stress Release

- A great way to help relieve the stress in your spine is to find the area of your life that requires structure and put it in place. It is amazing how fast the body will reflect the shifts you make energetically and emotionally.

- Another way to release stress in your spine is to work with a massage therapist. When they locate a tension spot, intuitively tune in to the source and let it go through the *"I don't have to do that anymore!"* technique.

The metaphysical body language I have shared with you here has come through self-observation and working with thousands of clients over the last

The Art of Self-Healing

30 years. This language is how I interpret the blockages in the body and how to release them.

Use this information as a guide. Use your intuition to open yourself up to infinite possibilities and discover your personal metaphysical body language. It may well be different to mine, but it will be a language you understand and can work with.

As with all things take what resonates. Push, pull and play with the tools and techniques offered up in this chapter, and experience them yourself.

Chapter Notes

The Art of Self-Healing

Chapter 6
How Do You Know If You Are Psychic?

One of the questions I'm most often asked is *"How do I know if I am psychic?"* The better question is *"How do I use my intuition?"*

Well, the thing is **everyone can sense things, whether it is about themselves or other people!**

To get to the truth about being psychic and intuitive I want to put aside the myth that some people are gifted with this ability and others are not. Everyone is born with the gift of intuition or as some would say a sixth sense.

I agree that some people are more aware of this gift than others and appear to be more talented; however **everyone** has the ability to develop their intuition to a heightened level. For most people, this takes practice.

It's important to say here that intuitively knowing things can be very frightening for a child, particularly if they have intuited something horrible happening to someone they know and love. For example, they have a knowing

The Art of Self-Healing

about a death or a catastrophe.

If a child speaks of this to their parents or someone they love and this person is not sensitive to the situation, or they themselves are afraid of this ability and answer negatively or harshly – the child may deliberately stop the development of this gift. In addition, most will likely not even remember they had the ability or experience as they grow into adulthood.

This is very sad.

I remember experiencing this situation as a 12 year old. Mrs Jones (not her real name), the lady across the road was very ill with kidney disease and was in hospital when we went on holidays. We were away for 5 weeks. A week before heading home, I wrote a postcard to her daughters and my friends saying I hoped their mum was recovering and was home from hospital.

That same night I had a dream. Mrs Jones appeared to me in the dream and somehow I knew she had died. In the morning I told Mum I didn't want to send the card because Mrs Jones had died the night before.

I remember being told to stop talking like that. Mum said, *"You couldn't know that, Julie! Stop telling lies."* I rarely argued with my mother, but I did argue with her this day and refused to send the card because I thought it would upset the girls to receive it after their mother had died.

We arrived home about 5 days later, and the first thing the middle daughter, Jenny (not her real name) did was run over to tell us that her mother had died on the night she appeared in my dream.

I said to Mum later, *"I told you she had died!"* She said, *"Yes, well, we won't talk about it now."*

It's important to explain why Mum didn't want to talk about this experience. As a child and a young married woman she had some disturbing experiences that left her frightened. She was so frightened she didn't want to hear about anything beyond our physical world and refused to discuss it until I started telling her I could see inside people's bodies when I was 25.

I don't recall the following event I'm sharing with you here, but my aunt who was there at the time reminded me of it some years ago.

Apparently, I was overheard saying to my sister, *"Mrs Smith (not her real name) killed her baby."* My sister's response was, *"No she didn't! She didn't have a baby."* At that time, I was too young to know about abortions, but the adult who overheard us talking knew. They told someone who told someone and it got back to Mrs Smith that I started the rumour.

It turned out to be true. However, only Mrs Smith and her doctor knew and that's the way she wanted it to stay. This is how the story was told to me – three pregnant women had contact with German measles (which we know can cause deafness and blindness in babies). Two of the women chose to keep their babies and they were born with these disabilities – and Mrs Smith chose to terminate. She was very angry that it became public knowledge.

It seems I was in a lot of trouble for revealing this information, albeit innocently.

Hearing stories like this, it is understandable why children shut down their natural gifts to avoid being punished or ridiculed.

In the 21st Century, parents are more aware of metaphysics and the gift of the sixth sense, in whatever form it takes, and many encourage their children to embrace their intuition rather than shut it down.

Congratulations and accolades to all those parents!

If you are a parent, I urge you to handle this situation sensitively and supportively. Don't turn it into something that is shameful, frightening or taboo.

The Problem - *Seeing and Feeling Ghosts*

Six year old Harry (not his real name) had been moody and difficult for some time and his mother was almost at her wits end when she randomly asked him if he sees ghosts. To her amazement he looked straight at her and said *"Yes"*.

He said he'd been seeing them for about 1½ years. There were many with mean red eyes. They were older and came to him when he closed his eyes. He didn't see them when his eyes were open, but he could feel and hear them – especially dinosaurs.

He also had images of his mother with her head cut off and his dead Nana with evil red eyes.

As you can imagine it was very frightening for him and his mother wasn't sure what to do.

The Solution – *The Magic Cylinder*

I asked Harry's mum to teach him how to protect himself with a magic cylinder that has a mirror on the outside. Each morning Harry imagined himself inside the cylinder and his mum helped him say a prayer of protection that went something like this.

> *"In the name of God, I ask that only the things for my highest good and safe passage through the day pass through the magic mirror and everything else is reflected back to where it came from in a safe way."*

This prayer can be embellished to make a child feel really safe. You could include extra protection by inviting their Guardian Angel inside the cylinder with them. You can also use colours inside the cylinder. Pink is the colour of love – and is always a great colour to use. You can give the colour a texture – it might be fine light mist or thick like a fog.

It's important to let the child be the creator of their magic cylinder so ensure you ask them what they want. You can give suggestions, but let it be their experience to manifest. If they want a different shape, that's fine, let it be whatever they create.

One of the other things I've noticed is that a connection with ghostly dimensions feeds on children's fear – if you can encourage children to become angry with the frightening ghosts, the connection becomes weak and eventually dissolves.

It is important to help children learn the difference between troublesome ghosts and helpful guides.

Whenever children feel afraid, I recommend they:

- Tell the ghosts to leave them alone;
- Use a mantra of "please God protect me"; and
- Imagine surrounding themselves with gold crosses.

The Result – Happy Child, Happy Mother

Harry said a lady in his dream killed all of the nasty ghosts except for one. He wasn't sure why she left one and was a little worried about this.

As well as following my instructions, he also asked for help from the angels and God.

I asked Harry to find out if the one left behind was a nasty ghost or a good one and explained that if it was a good one then he needed to make friends with it – as it would be one of his guides.

To do this, he imagined surrounding himself with gold crosses and invited the ghost into the space inside the gold crosses. I told Harry if the ghost was a good one it would be able to step into the space inside the crosses. Bad ghosts can't come into this protected area.

Harry met his Guardian Angel and she took away any further ghosts that were frightening him.

This was a fantastic outcome for Harry. He transformed from a moody, unsettled child into a happy and well-adjusted boy. However, it had been a frightening experience for his whole family.

This case made me wonder how many children carry trauma like this with them into their adult years.

Could this type of trauma be an explanation for some of the young suicides, not to mention psychiatric disorders?

If you are reading this and have been wondering whether you are psychic

The Art of Self-Healing

the answer is that you are definitely intuitive. Everyone born is intuitive.

The most important thing to remember is that you can develop your psychic gift through practice, <u>practice</u>, and more **practice**. By doing the exercises in this book and by experimenting yourself – you'll discover the mystery of the psychic and intuitive world.

Before long you will begin to **trust** your intuition. This is a vital key to being able to cross into the realm of intuitive healing. Trusting the information you intuit is the first step and the second step is to understand how to use that information to initiate self-healing.

To begin with you'll get impressions about things. This could be:

1. **Visually** – in your mind's eye or even with your eyes open (clairvoyance);
2. **Auditory** – you may hear with your inner ear or even with your human ear (clairaudience);
3. **Feeling** – you may simply experience a feeling in your body that you begin to recognise as having a specific meaning for you (clairsentience); and/or
4. **Knowing** – you have a clear knowing that something is correct, but you may be unable to back up your statement with facts or evidence (claircognizance).

I have read and also heard some metaphysical teachers say you are naturally stronger in one of these abilities than the others.

When I was told I had the gift of x-ray vision back in 1984, there wasn't a lot of information around like there is today, so, I didn't know about developing only one faculty. In fact, initially I was terrified of anything psychic or outside the physical world and didn't want anything to do with it.

As time went on I ended up having a lot to do with psychic development, intuition, metaphysics and exploring uncharted territory with my vibrational body. I developed all 4 psychic gifts equally because I didn't know it wasn't supposed to be possible.

The reason I'm telling you this story is so you don't presume you can only develop one faculty. With practice you can develop your intuition and all of your psychic faculties equally.

Chapter Notes

Chapter 7
Develop Your Psychic & Intuitive Gifts

Throughout this book there are exercises I encourage you to do. If you are serious about developing your insight and intuitive healing gifts, do all of these exercises over and over again.

It is important to start building new neural pathways to develop your abilities to the point where they become instinctive rather than strategic. Or another way of saying this is they become autonomic rather than deliberate.

You will often hear a judge in a competition saying to the contestants *"I can see you thinking"* however, when you are in the flow and working instinctively there is no evidence you are <u>thinking</u>.

The same will happen for you, BUT you do <u>need</u> to practice.

It's the same process as learning to crawl, to walk, to run, a new language, a new sport, a new anything you have to practice. As with learning anything new:

- you will have setbacks
- you will doubt yourself
- you will feel like a failure
- you will compare your results with others, and
- you will want to give up

The best advice I can give you is this, if you <u>WANT</u> to successfully use intuitive healing in your life, you need to practice. I practiced every day and even now still do something every day to keep my skills current. The interesting thing is – the more I practice, the more I want to practice.

I believe this is the first step to real change, so decide now whether you are going to do what it takes. **Remember, just wanting something is not enough - you need to take <u>ACTION</u>**.

Let's get started with developing your insight and intuitive healing skills.

Exercise: Journal

Get yourself a **journal** or a folder that can be used solely for your insight and intuitive healing development. There are two reasons for this:

(a) you will have a record of your development – this is important because as you grow you will forget how you felt and what your ability was like in the beginning. If you fall into the "doubt cycle" you'll forget how far you've come and your journal will act as your evidence

(b) you will be able to record your unique insights and what they mean for you. These insights will guide you to create and initiate self-healing templates unique for your situation

Visualisation

When I talk about visualisation, I refer to what you visualise in relation to the body.

My research has shown there are no rules about what you see; just know that when you see a vision or image it is related to intuiting or healing the root cause of what is going on for you in a particular area of your body.

I've also discovered the more "out there" your visions are the more powerful the results. What this means is **do not inhibit** your creativity when exploring this type of visualisation by wanting to see the literal image.

Visions may appear cryptic and need to be decoded so you can make sense of the imagery. This book helps you do that.

Visualisation is an important aspect of The Art of Self-Healing and healing yourself from within. However, in saying this it is not the only faculty that provides you with clues as to what is affecting your health and wellness.

You may also hear messages with your external ears and your internal ears or you may have a strong "gut feel" about your own health or someone you know.

Hearing voices doesn't happen very often for me, but it did happen when my father was having lung cancer surgery. I was at work while he was being operated on and whilst walking through a deserted lift well, I heard a masculine voice say *"The operation was a success, but the patient died."* I spun around to see who had spoken, but there was no one there.

My father did survive the operation, but five days later due to complications the family unanimously asked the doctor to turn off his life support.

Dad continued to breathe unaided through the day, but his vital signs slowly faded as time went on. A couple of hours before he died, I was wondering when would be the moment of transition.

The same masculine voice said, *"He will die at 5pm."* Incredibly, the heart monitor connected to Dad flat-lined at 5pm indicating he had crossed-over. Where did the voice come from? I don't know. Did it help? Yes, it did.

Do the exercises throughout the book and you will naturally increase your psychic and intuitive ability.

Chapter Notes

Chapter 8
How Insight and Intuition Can Help

What's the "P" Factor?

The "P" Factor is a combination of technical and traditional healing skills that accentuate your natural gifts. Remember, everyone is intuitive, even you. The biggest thing I hear about intuition is DOUBT. Because intuition is an intangible (it can't be seen) – left brain (scientific) oriented people particularly doubt or are skeptical about it.

If you are predominantly left brain orientated, having the "P" Factor may be challenging.

However, **you can** awaken your intuition and **you can** develop your psychic skills through regular practice. If you want to have the "P" Factor I recommend you practice every day for at least for 10 minutes. More is better!

Intuition practice is similar to going to the gym, if you go once a week for an hour you don't see a lot of result, even though you've put in that much effort. However, if you go to the gym for 15 minutes a day, even though it is a short workout, you have consistency and will see better tangible results over time.

The more you exercise the more you want to exercise.

The last piece of the puzzle for the "P" Factor is to develop **YOUR** gift, the gift that is unique to you. The rebel in me says don't blindly follow someone else's gift and expect to have the same results. Use the teachings of others, me included, and morph that teaching into what feels authentic for you and your gift.

This will make you feel authentic. You will resonate with your insights and intuition and get tangible results with your self-healing.

Find the root cause of illness and disease

In quantum physics the deeper you explore the atom the more you discover its energy. The atom has an invisible force field that sends out waves of electrical energy.

Those energy waves can be measured and you can see the effects, but they are not a material or tangible reality. They have no substance because they are simply electricity.

Thoughts and emotions are not tangible, but they are energy and they are felt tangibly in the body. You can't see the wind, but you can see the effects of the wind when the trees move. Similarly you feel the wind on your skin. You can't see it, but you feel it.

There are positive, uplifting thoughts and emotions and there are negative, degenerating thoughts and emotions.

Both types are experienced by everyone at some point in their life and different facets of your life are more vulnerable to the spectrum of emotions.

Why?

Because you have a blockage or energy is trapped and doesn't flow freely.

How insight and intuition can help

If you don't attend to the blockage early the energy becomes denser and builds up to the point where it becomes a physical blockage which manifests as discomfort, illness or disease.

It is also true that our health is linked to the food we eat, what we drink, the environment we live in, the way we are born, accidents and a variety of other triggers.

Let's look a bit deeper into health and wellbeing and consider the concept of past and future lives of the one soul.

I believe illness or disease is the result of thoughts and emotions throughout the continuum of your stream of time. When a baby is born with illness or disease this is a hard situation to understand or reconcile.

Is there a best way of viewing this? I don't know. In my mind, we don't know what a soul has experienced prior to being born and what vibrations have been brought forward nor what that soul wants to experience in any given life.

Thoughts and emotions also impact on the choices you make, particularly in relation to the food you eat and the environment you surround yourself with. Thoughts and emotions can aggravate your stress levels which impact your immune system. The immune system is the powerhouse that keeps your body healthy.

There is a belief around releasing blocked emotion that says you need to relive the experience that caused the blockage.

I don't believe this!

Not just one incident causes trapped emotion, it is a series of incidents that create layers of emotion. If you accept the concept of past lives (as I do) then you believe it carries on through lifetimes. Rather than unpacking each layer and run the risk of anchoring that blockage further into the body and psyche, it is better to work with the pattern that creates the layer.

I have long been criticised for starting projects and not finishing them. I would get to 97% complete and then walk away. It seemed to be a case of Fear of Success. During a hypnosis session, the therapist asked me "*What is the worst that could happen?*"

I was instantly transported to another time zone. This was not just witnessing a vision, I was experiencing the moment in real time.

It was a cold, miserable day in England during the 19th Century. I was standing under cover of a sandstone walkway looking out at the rain with my husband. I recognized him as someone from my present life. I would love to have married him, but something stopped me exploring that possibility. During this session, I discovered why.

We were part of the aristocracy. He was wearing a suit and top hat and looked very handsome, even in his anger with me. I wore a beautiful powder blue gown with a bustle and matching bonnet. The conversation was not a happy one.

I wanted to start my own business. My husband said, "*No wife of mine is going to work or own a business. If you go ahead with your plans you are no longer my wife and will lose all the benefits our marriage brings with it.*"

This decision must have been very important to me, as I chose the business. Unfortunately, I got sick and died within 4 months of starting the business.

So the answer to the therapist's question was, "*I will die!*"

By discovering this emotional block and limiting belief whilst under hypnosis, I was able to dissolve it. Perhaps my soul had experienced other "evidence" in other life times that if I was successful I would die. I don't know.

What I do know is that since this hypnosis session, I have been able to complete projects, my business has flourished and I feel successful.

It is important to go to the root of the blockage and clear it there. You don't need to rehash all the stories confirming the "evidence" of the limiting belief and unlock the stories one at a time.

When you work with the pattern, rather than the story, you can clear lifetimes of trapped emotion.

How to locate your authentic self in the Divine Stream

The best way for me to explain this is to tell a story.

A few years ago, I randomly watched Oprah. I didn't know it at the time, but that day I discovered the first clue to being my authentic self.

A guest on Oprah ran an experiment with about 30 people who went to their jobs for a week with a notebook. The notebook had a red cover on one side and a green cover on the other side. All the tasks they did during the day which uplifted their energy were written on the green side of the notebook, and all the tasks which deflated their energy they wrote on the red side.

The end result was a visual record of how much their job was affecting their wellbeing in a positive or negative way.

The tasks that uplift you are your strengths and the tasks that deflate you are your weaknesses.

Many people believe they have to focus their attention on transforming their weaknesses to achieve balance.

What I learned that day was to focus on and heighten my strengths (the things that strengthen my energy) and get someone else to do the things that weaken my energy (and even better, find people whose strengths are my weaknesses to help with this).

This was a profound revelation as I can do many things with excellent skill, but some of these skills weaken my energy. When I discovered the things I excel at are not necessarily my strengths, a huge weight lifted from my shoulders and a new exceptional chapter of my life began.

In fact, some of the things where your skill level is average can actually be your strengths because they uplift your energy. The opposite is also true; the things you excel at can be your weaknesses. Something to think about!

From that moment, I began the metamorphosis to being my authentic self.

The next biggest shift happened when I integrated my two lives – the corporate | straight, conventional personality and the metaphysical | inter-dimensional traveler personality. Two distinct people, at least they were in my mind!

At last, I had the courage to be "ME" and really understood "not everyone has to like me". It's true; I wanted everyone to like me! This can be debilitating. By being my authentic self, I now attract into my life the people who want to work with and spend time with me and they like me just the way I am! Warts and all!

Now, that is a powerful lesson!

By being your authentic self you will polarise people and that's okay! Polarising people means that some will love you and some won't like you at all because you push their buttons in a reactive way. Be prepared for this to happen when you put on your authentic cloak and proudly step out into the world as "YOU".

Exercise: Strengths and Weaknesses

- Take a notebook around with you for a week – it doesn't need to have red and green on the cover. Write down all the things you do that uplifts and deflates your energy and at the end of the week review your findings. Once you know what your true strengths and weaknesses are, make plans to outsource your weaknesses and magnify your strengths. This may not happen overnight, however, to live your authentic life you have to start somewhere so it may as well be here.

- It is a good idea to get yourself an accountability buddy who will support you to create these shifts in your life.

- **NOTE:** This exercise does not mean you leave your job, struggle financially and create unnecessary hardship. This is an invitation to observe your strengths and weaknesses, understand yourself more and plan the transformation of your life by managing your energy

How insight and intuition can help

better. It may even create an opportunity for your job description to be restructured so your strengths benefit your business or your employer's business.

Feel good about yourself

It's a sad reality that many people are negatively limited by their beliefs, subconscious blockages and trapped emotions.

I put my hand up and admit to being riddled with emotional blockages in the past. Are they completely gone? No, but much has been released over the past 15 years and more particularly the past 3 years.

How do I know and how can you know for yourself? There are a number of elements to give you this clarity.

(a) Firstly, your day to day **emotional wellbeing** is above the Amnesia Line® more than it is below it

(b) You frequently experience **synchronicity** (2 or more events happening at the same time which are not causally related, but have meaning together) and **serendipity** (a pleasant unexpected happening) which brings an added dimension of joy and wonder to your world

(c) You experience being in **"the flow"** – everything seems to unfold easily and effortlessly or put another way you are manifesting what you want in your life when you want it

Life has a rhythm of ups and downs or peaks and valleys. This is not unique to you or me. Everyone lives life to the rhythm of this dance. It depends on where your Amnesia Line® sits on this pattern that determines how well you cope with life's curve balls.

The Amnesia Line® is a concept I developed to explain to my clients why things can go pear shaped in life and at other times everything flows. When you go below the line you forget all the resources you have to manage the bumpy ride we call life.

The Art of Self-Healing

When you are above the line you magically know what to do and when to do it making life feel easy and effortless. You seem to live with purpose, cope with disasters and have fun.

So how can you live in "the flow", feel good about yourself and experience wonder at the magic and majesty of life each day?

Exercise: How To Stay Above The Amnesia Line®

- Make a list of 10 things you love to do that make you happy, calm, peaceful, centered, rejuvenated, relaxed.

- Write the list on the back of an old business card and put it somewhere you will see it when you need it.

- Here's my list:
    1. Paint
    2. Draw
    3. Read trashy novels
    4. Make sacred art from ripped paper
    5. Go for a bush walk
    6. Listen to music
    7. Call a friend
    8. Go to the movies
    9. Re-arrange the furniture
    10. Take photographs

Why have I asked you to write these things down? You may find this hard to believe, but when you go below the line you forget all the amazing things you love to do that make you happy and help you cope with life.

You may need to do more than one activity to breakthrough and move back above the Amnesia Line®. The secret to getting back above the line is to take action. Any action – you need to get the energy moving, so do something you know historically makes you happy.

How insight and intuition can help

Living in the flow

Here are some of the ways you can help yourself to live in the flow:

- Proactively work on yourself to release limiting beliefs and emotional blockages. Here's some ways to do this:
    - Work with a **practitioner** who has a gift in this type of work
    - Work with a **coach** who holds you accountable
    - Work with a **mentor** who has walked the journey before you
    - Become the **observer** of your patterns – when you recognise what you do and understand it, you'll notice the activities triggering the pattern will fall away (albeit revealing a different pattern, for you to observe and understand – and the process goes on)
    - **Read** personal development, spiritual, metaphysical, quantum physics books that educate, inspire and uplift you
    - **Spend time** with people who inspire and uplift you and protect your energy from the people who deflate you
- Take **responsibility** for your thoughts, speech, actions and intentions:
    - **Florence Scovel Shinn** – an extraordinary woman from the early 20th century wrote several books about this. I recommend you get her books and take the time to read and understand her message. Particularly – *"The Game of Life"*, *"Your Word is Your Wand"* and *"The Power of the Spoken Word"*
    - **Lynne McTaggart** – if you are predominantly left brained, or need scientific evidence of metaphysics and the intangible, I highly recommend you read Lynne's book, *"The Intention Experiment"*. Some say it doesn't have flow, and it is a whole bunch of research thrown together in a book and this may be so, but you will hopefully discover as I did, the genius thread of pulling all this research together and gain an understanding

about the power of your intentions. It really is an extraordinary composition of scientific research into the intangible.

- **David Wilcock** – David's book *"The Hidden Science of Lost Civilisations"* is a very interesting read. It is along the lines of Lynne McTaggart's work, but more focused on the 2012 calendar mystery. This book, which took me a few months to read, sparked a number of extraordinary new healing templates.

- **Meditate** regularly. There are many different forms of meditation, so explore them all and find one that works for you. I read recently that the top entrepreneurs in the world all meditate in some way. So if you think about it, meditation gives you the edge!

- My favourite quick meditation is to sit quietly for 15 minutes and focus on an imaginary light in a tunnel. No extensive visualising, no focusing on my breath, no counting mala beads or repeating a mantra and when the mind wanders, simply come back to the light in the tunnel. I find this calming and centering - try it and you may find it will calm and centre you, too.

- **Breakthrough Feeling art** – this is an activity where you drop into "the moment". All the chatter of day-to-day life recedes and disappears for a time, allowing you to rejuvenate and restore your reservoir of available energy. I personally create collages of ripped paper. A gardener will potter in the garden. A mechanic will tinker with an engine. There are no rules about what you do, but do something!

How to manage the expectations of others and yourself?

Exercise: Say "No"

- Say "NO" when you want to say "NO".

- Although, in saying that, you will need to use some discernment in your job and your unique life responsibilities.

If you have a job that requires you to do tasks that you really don't want to do (and they deflate your energy), you may need to find another job or do the tasks you are paid to do, but change the way you think and feel about them.

One way I am able to do this is to think of the jobs/tasks I **don't want** to do, but really **need** to do, as an act of service and contemplate the Divine Being as I do them.

If you have children and/or pets you are responsible for, at times you will have to do things you don't want to do.

Again I recommend you shift the focus from imposition to service.

However, if there are things you NEED to do because you are responsible for them and they are causing you to struggle emotionally, physically, mentally or spiritually, **ask for help**. But don't be surprised when some people say "NO".

It doesn't mean you don't deserve to get help. The people who say "NO" are looking after their balance of energy (whether this is being done consciously or unconsciously).

Keep asking till you find someone who has the capacity to help you. Ask in a heart-felt, conscious way, not in a demanding, unconscious way. The outcome will always be more positive.

Have you noticed how difficult people find it to ask for and accept help? I wonder if this is a key factor in the rise of depression.

How do you heal all of the bodies?

It is complicated, but here is a good start:

- **Physically:** Eat healthy nutritious food, exercise regularly and get adequate sleep
- **Emotionally:** Acknowledge your feelings. Feelings are neither good nor bad; they are just what you feel in that moment. Keep a journal

of your feelings and write from the position of the observer. Release emotional blockages regularly. This doesn't mean you have a big vomit of emotional garbage all over someone who cares about you. Instead release the emotion trapped in your body using the processes in this book or work with a practitioner gifted in this area.

- **Mentally:** Thoughts shape who you are, so be responsible for them. Apart from sleeping, allocate non-thinking time in your day. This can be done through yoga, listening to music, anything really where you can drop into a feeling place, rather than a thinking place. The intention is to give your mind a break.

- **Spiritually:** Have sacred time where you connect with God, the Divine, the Universe. This connection may be called something different for each person, but do it. You can meditate, go to church, pray, spend time in nature, create sacred art. Essentially, this is a time when you are alone with the magnificent spark that ignites the life in each cell of your body. Consciously and deliberately connect with it.

Underlying all of this is HOPE, so find it and nurture it.

Elevate to a higher level of consciousness

Have you heard the saying, *"You can't change anyone but yourself!"* even though you may desperately want to change someone else!

I tried for 20 years to change my husband – it's no wonder we struggled during this time. Then I went on a 4 week spiritual retreat and came home with the cellular understanding that my husband was just fine the way he was. I finally understood I am only responsible for me and my actions – physically, mentally, emotionally and spiritually. Amazingly the dynamics shifted profoundly. We've had happy years since!

If you want to raise your level of consciousness it takes consistent inner work. This book is a great help to get you started. However, you may find that regularly working with a practitioner will help you grow more quickly and with more profound insights.

How insight and intuition can help

Wouldn't it be amazing to live in the Joy or Peace vibration permanently! We can help you do this. Learn more in the last chapter.

Chapter Notes

Chapter 9
8 Key Qualities of Intuitive Insight

These are the 8 key qualities that support the development of strong intuitive insight:

(a)   Empathy

(b)   Discernment

(c)   Compassion

(d)   Strength

(e)   Intuition

(f)   Trust

(g)   Ethics

(h)   Authentic

What is empathy?

The Oxford Dictionary states that the definition of empathy is *"the ability to understand and share the feelings of another"*.

As an intuitive and/or empath it is important you understand the feelings of others without feeling pity or sorrow for their circumstances. The gift of empathy opens you to great insight into what's happening for others emotionally. However, it is important to observe the emotions of others, rather than diving into the pond of emotion with them.

Empathy for others will give you an understanding of what it is like to walk in their shoes, even if it is only a little hint of what they are experiencing. It will be enough for you to support them in a non-emotional or judgmental way.

Don't confuse empathy with sympathy!

According to the Oxford Dictionary sympathy means *"Feelings of pity and sorrow for someone else's misfortune"*.

Below is my understanding of the difference between empathy and sympathy.

When you **empathise** you feel what others are experiencing to the point of understanding their emotions in relation to their circumstance, but you don't go down the rabbit hole of drama with them.

When you **sympathise**, not only do you understand the emotions, you personally experience it as you jump into the whirlpool with them and your energy spirals out of control like theirs. This doesn't help you or them in a constructive way.

When you understand this distinction and focus on empathy rather than sympathy, the negative feelings associated with sympathy don't happen.

I personally struggled with this distinction for decades. Being sympathetic rather than empathetic most likely contributed to the many illnesses I created in my 30s and 40s.

Thankfully I understand this distinction better now. This understanding came about through one of my mentors, Andrew Grant, explaining it and then me consistently working at integrating the distinction into my unconscious competence.

Now that you have wisdom about this distinction, I encourage you to consciously work on integrating empathy into your day-to-day life and leave sympathy alone.

It is also important to understand the impact of having too much empathy, or being a natural empath.

If you can't turn your empathy switch off you will continue to feel the thoughts, emotions and physical symptoms of all and sundry. I have met people who describe this as the "empathy curse", rather than the great gift it can be.

Exercise: How to handle too much empathy

There are many well-known ways of protecting your energy and handling your empath gift such as:

- A Prayer of Protection see page 28 for my prayer.
- **White light** yourself imagine you are surrounded by white light.
- Put yourself inside a protective box or cylinder – see page 25.
- **Aromatherapy** burning essential oils to cleanse the room and protect your energy; wear the oils on your body.
- **Aura Soma** is a form of colour healing therapy which works on the aura.
- **Singing bowl** use a singing bowl to transform the energy in your workplace, home and around you.
- And many other techniques not explored in this book.

All of the above techniques are great, but if your empath gift is driving you nuts and you just want to be **"normal"**, the following solution may work for you.

How to turn your Empath Gift On and Off

Over recent years, I've been hearing more and more people describe their empath ability as a curse. They want to know how to turn it off.

We are like radio receivers as well as radio transmitters and it's the receiving element that sometimes needs to be tuned out. Below is a process I used with a client that is designed to help turn off your empath switch.

Exercise: Empath Radio Dial

- Take the time to meditate and visualise the dial of an old radio. If you are an empath it is likely your dial will be continually roaming and tuning into the closest frequency, giving you no rest and respite from the thoughts and feelings of others.

- Turn the dial to static and lock it in. You can turn it down eg., from 10 to 1, or turn it hard to the left or right and lock it in by pushing the dial into the radio or pulling it out till it clicks. When you want to be empathic release the dial back to free movement and allow it to scan frequencies again.

- I've shared the concept here, now you can transform the concept into your version of the "Radio Dial". The more creative you are the more profound the impact will be on all your bodies.

Responsibility For Other People's Stuff

It's not "your fault" if someone is in crisis mode, so it is not your responsibility to fix it or rescue them. As a friend you can be objective, feel empathy and if **asked** offer any practical solutions you see from an objective perspective, however, it is up to them as to whether or not they accept it.

A great rule of thumb is to only offer advice if it is sought and have no expectation of it being followed.

If someone chooses to reject your advice, know that it is NOT a reflection of their feelings about you as a person. Instead, they are making a choice about how they will handle **their** crisis. The truth is that each one of us needs to make decisions based on our own intuition, insight, education and feelings, not blindly follow what someone else tells us to do.

This was a huge challenge for me to understand and accept as it is so easy to feel wounded by the words and actions of another person. Often I felt my insights and intuition were accurate, yet they were being ignored time and time again with consequences that could have been avoided.

I took this personally and felt rejected and betrayed. What I have learned is this – what someone takes from their crises (lessons) is their business. And what someone takes from insight and intuition about these lessons (theirs or another's) is also their business.

Have you noticed the same pattern of crisis repeating itself in your life and each time the consequence is magnified? It's almost like the Universe is saying *"Have you got it yet??? NO??? Then here's some more drama. Do you get it, now???"*

It is similar to trying to explain a concept to a child. If they don't get it the first time you try to explain it in another way and then another way, ultimately expecting that they will understand. You could try 5 different ways before there is a glint of understanding. The more you try the more exaggerated you make the delivery in your attempt to make them understand.

Here is a pattern I perpetuated till I understood what I was doing.

One of the patterns I kept repeating in my life was with men who would convince me of the opposite of what I knew to be true. I allowed these men to invalidate my intuition repeatedly. Sometimes this led to me making decisions that led us to financial hardship.

Why did I allow this? Because I believed (my limiting belief) they knew better than me and that my intuition was not valuable. Hence effectively invalidating my intuition.

When I recognised this pattern fully, I stopped being confused by strong male energy (the energy I was lacking) and now I trust my intuition. I still get tested, but I recognise the signs and make better choices.

Did I need to experience so many crises around this pattern before I recognized it? I'll never know. However, I do know that the consequence of recognising it, understanding myself better and integrating this learning into my life has gifted me with super-heightened intuition.

I notice and experience doubt every now and then and I have the resources to transform it quickly.

This took disciplined commitment to self-understanding. Are you prepared to invest in yourself to remove doubt from your world?

I love the following story which came to me by email. I don't know who wrote it, but is well worth a read and seriously consider the implications of the message.

Things Aren't Always What They Seem

Two traveling angels stopped to spend the night in the home of a wealthy family. The family was rude and refused to let the angels stay in the mansion's guest room.

Instead the angels were given a small space in the cold basement. As they made their bed on the hard floor, the older angel saw a hole in the wall and repaired it.

When the younger angel asked why, the older angel replied, *"Things aren't always what they seem"*.

The next night the pair came to rest at the house of a very poor, but very hospitable farmer and his wife. After sharing what little food they had the couple let the angels sleep in their bed where they could have a good night's rest.

When the sun came up the next morning the angels found the farmer and his wife in tears. Their only cow, whose milk had been their sole income, lay dead in the field.

The younger angel was infuriated and asked the older angel, *"How could you have let this happen? The first man had everything, yet you helped him!"* she accused.

"The second family had little, but was willing to share everything, and you let the cow die."

"Things aren't always what they seem," the older angel replied.

8 Key qualities of intuitive insight

"When we stayed in the basement of the mansion, I noticed there was gold stored in that hole in the wall. Since the owner was so obsessed with greed and unwilling to share his good fortune, I sealed the wall so he wouldn't find it. Then last night as we slept in the farmer's bed, the angel of death came for his wife ... I gave him the cow instead. **Things aren't always what they seem**!"

What does this all mean?

All is not what it seems – look at the metaphors within your life and self-understanding will sparkle in your consciousness more clearly.

It is good to reflect on your life, particularly the challenging times, as this is when you had to dig deep into your inner reservoir and locate your strength. It is in reflection that you discover how much those times shaped you to be the amazing person you are today.

When you see your family or friends struggling with a crisis, often all they need is an ear to listen as they unravel the solution themselves. Don't offer advice or a solution unless they specifically ask you to. Unwanted advice creates many problems for all concerned.

The best way to determine whether you should say something is ask yourself if you would like someone to give you unsolicited advice. Ask permission first is a good principle to follow when giving advice.

What is discernment?

Discernment is the ability to determine the value and quality of a subject or event. More particularly it is the ability to look beyond the physical view and make a detailed judgment about that "thing". In relation to a virtue or quality of your personality, if you are a discerning individual, you are considered to possess wisdom and good judgment.

It is important for you to discern with wisdom and demonstrate good judgment when using your intuition.

If you don't know something, say so, don't guess. However, do listen to your intuition. One of the things I have experienced personally and hear from others is that intuition is so fleeting it can be missed completely or brushed off as of no consequence.

To heighten your quality of discernment again you must observe yourself. Notice the fleeting messages that caress your psyche, and grab them into your consciousness like a gecko catching a moth.

This will raise your level of sensitivity to receiving information, thereby benefiting you and others. The wisdom element of this quality is what you do with the knowledge you receive.

I have found that wisdom comes through making choices which can feel right or good and wrong or bad. However this is not true – these choices are simply choices – neither right nor wrong or good nor bad. Choices are an opportunity to experience and learn. Your task is to learn from all experiences and have the intention to make the best choice you can with the information you have at hand.

What is compassion?

The Oxford dictionary meaning of compassion is *sympathetic pity and concern for the sufferings or misfortunes of others.*

Earlier in this chapter I talked about the difference between empathy and sympathy. In line with this I don't recommend you drop into the feeling of deep sympathy with others as you will enter the downward spiral with them. However, if you have a strong desire to alleviate another's suffering there is a **HUGE BUT!!!**

Do so only if they want to be relieved of their suffering!!!

It is really important to have permission from people before your strong desire to alleviate the suffering of others is put into action.

This can be hard, especially if you are naturally a giving, solution oriented person?

VERY HARD!!!

Practice the discipline of asking first and watch what happens.

Sometimes I discover that even when a client comes to me and pays good money to be helped, underlying this conscious desire to be helped, there is a subconscious resistance. This is where the real work begins.

Through practice, wisdom and intuition it is possible to communicate with the subconscious and gain permission. However, this process is not something I can teach in this book. Go to medicalintuitionacademy.com – where you will find the details on how you can learn more about this.

If you cannot get permission from the subconscious to work with this resistance it is best to do nothing.

The keys to having excellent strength

The word strength can be broken down into the following areas and each area illustrates a different type of strength.

- energetic strength
- physical strength and stamina
- tough love
- boundaries
- discipline and resilience.

Energetic Strength

This was a challenging strength for me to articulate and so I engaged in a lot of research to further my knowledge.

The results of my study have led me to the Zen Forum – www.zenforuminternational.org whose information helped me to clarify the definition of energetic strength.

I mentioned earlier about digging deep into your inner reservoir to locate your strength. Let me use the metaphor of the inner reservoir as a way of describing the location of your energetic strength.

The Art of Self-Healing

If the reservoir is full you have a great capacity for self-understanding, insights, transmitting this strength through your gifts whether it is food (if you are a chef), healing hands, your voice or your whole body radiance.

Have you heard these words -*"your life force is weak"*?

In 1995, I became very unwell. For 12 months I helped people around the world 7 days a week because I thought it was my responsibility to give if they asked. The truth is I had no boundaries.

It is difficult to describe the illness. My inner reservoir was completely empty. This still brings up deep emotion and I wonder *"How could I have let that happen?"*

One day in October 1995, I couldn't function physically so I phoned work to say I wouldn't be in as I was sick. Interestingly, my friend and doctor rang my workplace to speak to me that particular day. He knew I went to work regardless of how unwell I felt, so he called me at home to ask what was wrong.

I said, *"I feel as if someone has pulled the plug out and drained my energy. I'm so exhausted!"*

"Can you drive to my clinic?"

"Yes. I'll come now."

To be honest, I don't know how I got to the clinic. Once there, he gave me intravenous Vit C and Vit B complex which helped a little. He told me I was dangerously ill.

I drove home and Frank arrived not long after I returned to find me lying on the sofa. He asked, *"Why aren't you at work?"* He also knew I went to work regardless of how I felt.

He sat with me on the sofa and I explained how I just wanted to find a hole, crawl in it and die. In his loving way he looked at me and said, *"Well you can't. You have 2 children to look after!"*

I could feel a tremendous pulling towards the ceiling. I looked up to find a hole had opened up in the ceiling and arms were reaching down for me. I floated out of my body and lost consciousness.

Frank woke me 3 hours later and reminded me that I had an acupuncturist appointment and I should go.

Feeling like a space cadet and not quite in my body, I somehow managed the drive to the acupuncturist's clinic.

My acupuncturist, Jim, felt my pulses and looked at me stunned, *"You have no discernible chi energy in your body! I'm going to give you some with these needles and you are NOT to use this energy on anyone else!"*

I was Jim's last patient for the day and he sat with me after he put the acupuncture needles into my body. In utter exhaustion my eyes closed, I lay on the table and felt the needles weave their healing magic.

After 20 minutes I was compelled to open my eyes. I was stunned by a vision on the ceiling. A bright light was hovering above me and I could see Jesus within the light. His hand reached down out of the light and rested on my heart.

All the tension left my body and I felt peaceful.

I turned to Jim and asked him if he had felt anything change in the room. He said, *"I have just had the most incredible peace wash over me."*

I told him what had just happened with Jesus appearing and he said, *"You are going to get better."*

Jesus appeared many more times during my treatment.

Jim saved my life. After 6 months of intensive acupuncture treatment he said, *"I didn't think you would make it."* I believe the extra help we got from Jesus pulled me through.

What I did to my inner reservoir was terrible. I didn't understand the potential danger of neglecting to look after and nurture this vital resource.

You don't have to personally experience a disaster like this to learn a lesson; if you can learn this lesson through my appalling neglect it will have served a Divine purpose.

Energetic strength can also be described as the flame of vitality that shines in your heart. Others can light this flame if it goes out, but they can't keep the flame alight for you. This is your responsibility.

This flame is fueled internally through self-understanding, discipline, energetic boundaries, living with passion and purpose, having daily devotional/sacred time to centre "you" in the flame, studying life, learning the ways of spirituality and allowing yourself to be inspired daily.

These are some of the ways to keep your flame alight; however, there are as many ways as there are unique individuals. Consider this:

What do you currently do or could you do to fuel your flame and fill your inner reservoir with energetic strength?

Physical Strength and Stamina

The less you do with your body, the less you are capable of doing with it.

To have physical strength and stamina, you need to move your body. There are many ways of doing this:

- go for a walk 3-4 times a week
- yoga, tai-chi, pilates
- martial arts
- sport
- gym workout
- exercise classes.

My favourite ways to move my body are walking and pilates.

If you have a physical restriction on moving your body, get some advice from a professional who will support you with a unique program for you. Regular movement is essential for this goal.

Tough Love

Does hearing the words *"tough love"* make you cringe inside?

It does me, yet when I think back over my life it is when tough love has been administered by friends, family, mentors or a random person I didn't even know that I realise that's when I made a huge jump in self-understanding.

Did I like it? **NO!**

Did I benefit from it? **YES!**

What do I mean by tough love?

The Oxford dictionary says this: *"Promotion of a person's welfare, especially that of an addict, child, or criminal, by enforcing certain constraints on them, or requiring them to take responsibility for their actions."*

However, in the context of this book, when I talk about tough love it is about being held accountable for your actions, not necessarily in relation to an addiction.

If you are on the receiving end of tough love (and I am not talking about being bullied here) you may feel that life is "not fair" and you ask yourself questions like *"Why are you doing this to me? You don't love me!"*

My question to you is this – *"Have you really considered your situation through the eyes of the person giving the tough love to understand why this may be happening?"*

Here's the thing, life can be tough or can appear to be tough. The best way I've found to manage this is to inspect what I have done to create the chaos. I don't always find THE best answer, but I do find plenty to consider.

My point is this, if you are experiencing tough love, instead of reacting to it contemplate and consider the reason for it. Wisdom comes to us in many guises. A diamond is created through tremendous pressure – perhaps this is a time of creating your inner diamond.

If you are administering tough love and it is coming from the heart – and not via the ego in a malicious, vindictive, hurtful way – stay strong in your conviction that you are providing an invaluable service to the other person involved. However, be mindful of overstepping their boundaries. If someone asks for advice, if you are able to help do so, if you don't know, say so. Unsolicited advice is rarely welcome. If you want to give advice, ask permission first and don't be surprised if the answer is no.

Boundaries

There are many meanings of the word "boundaries", however, in this instance I am talking about the boundaries you make in relation to your values and your energy distribution.

It's about what you will and won't do and what you are willing to accept as part of your world.

You may also hear people talk about having "weak boundaries". When I think about this term – I'm sad that I didn't understand what this meant when I began my journey into metaphysics.

However, if I hadn't experienced weak boundaries I wouldn't be able to make this point now to help you.

The following is my interpretation of **weak boundaries**:

- **Not knowing** who you are.
- **Losing your identity** in the strong personality of another (eg., partner, friend or work colleague).
- **Not** having **alone time** (this is quite distinct from being lonely).
- Allowing others to **impose** on your generous nature.
- Being the **doormat** that everyone wipes their shoes on (metaphorically).
- **Releasing more** from your inner reservoir **than you put into it.**
- In other words giving more than you receive – and I don't mean tangible things – I mean energetic and emotional gifts.

- **Continuing to give** when there is little left to give.
- Saying **YES** when you mean **NO**.

The following is my interpretation of **strong boundaries**:

- **Knowing who you are** – this is a continual self-education, self-observation and self-awareness process.
- Maintain your **unique identity** in all relationships.
- Making time for you to have **alone time** – time where you meditate, read, do sacred art, contemplate, listen to music or be transported into other realms.
- **Give** to others only **when you have the energetic capacity** – and say NO when you mean NO.
- Be **fully present** in all activities.
- **Refill your inner reservoir** regularly – like watering the garden to create a beautiful environment.

Learning Through Miss-takes

When I started this journey I didn't understand any of the above. I was very naïve and learned through my mistakes.

When I went on the TV show "The Extraordinary" in 1994, tens of thousands of people contacted me from around the world seeking my help. It was completely overwhelming. My telephone didn't stop ringing for 3 years and we had to take a huge bag to the post office to collect the mail every few days.

I erroneously believed that if people asked me to help them I was obliged to help, even if it was to the detriment of my health and energy.

At this time, I had no mentors and felt like I was swimming in a dark pond with little external guidance.

I wanted people to like me and I craved being needed. I thought if I gave enough of me then I wouldn't disappoint others or create conflict.

Not true!!!!

The consequence of this ignorance – and very weak boundaries – was that I created 4 thyroid diseases (and ultimately lost my voice for 12 months); rotted most of the body parts that you can afford to lose and had to have them removed.

Since having thyroid cancer surgery in 2000 and recovering my voice in 2001, I live my life with stronger boundaries which I have progressively built upon. This didn't happen overnight and I had to work hard to release old behaviour patterns and create new ones.

The result of this persistence for strong boundaries is that my body is healthy and I have stopped growing tumours.

Discipline and Resilience

It takes discipline to be strong physically, mentally, emotionally and spiritually.

Ask anyone who is strong in each or all of these areas and they'll validate this statement.

Sometimes it can feel like all your hard work is swept out from under your feet in one huge smack. I've been there too, but what I've discovered is this – decide right here and right now to dig deep into your metaphysical and spiritual practice and your discipline will carry you through.

Life is filled with disappointments, trials and challenges. The way I have been taught to deal with this (and which I really resonate with) is that "stuff" happens to the outer construct, but the inner being, your spirit can only be affected by this "stuff" if you give it permission to affect you.

Refuse To Be Broken

The following story gives an example of how people can refuse to let their spirit be broken. A Japanese prisoner of war had this attitude and said, "*You can take away all of my liberties but you can't have my spirit."* Every day he played a game of golf in his mind to keep his spirit nourished. The amazing thing was that he survived the war and came home with a better handicap than when he left. He had not played one physical game of golf in that time.

There are other amazing stories about Jews in the concentration camps in Europe who survived when all those around them were gassed. I believe these survivors had resilience ignited deep in their spirit protecting them from physical harm.

Read James Redfield's *Celestine Prophecy* series to get a better understanding of how you can protect yourself from harm with your energy and connection to Divine Source. I'm a huge fan of these books and love the parable learning style James used to deliver his message.

From personal experience, I know it takes discipline and practice to locate this resilience and nourish it.

Something to think about – Are you nourishing and strengthening your spirit?

Remember intuition?

Let's remind ourselves about what intuition means:
Intuition is an instinctive response that comes before your left brain rationalises or interferes with it. This response generates a tangible sensation in your body (you may not have identified yours yet, but I'll show you how in this section if you haven't). Intuition says that what you are thinking and/or feeling is accurate and to trust it even though there is no evidence to support your instinct except for your physical response (eg., goosebumps) and inner knowing.

Your instinctive response arrives without you having to think about it. This is the speed of knowing. It is a heart response and I call it "authentic knowing". When you experience this knowing you are feeling it at a cellular level and you become conscious of your body vibrating in response to the truth.

Sometimes I describe this as my "Moet Moment" as it can literally feel like champagne zinging through your blood or you may simply be conscious of it as a vibration.

How do you develop intuition?

Initially, it is simply being willing to connect into your feeling body and develop that neural pathway.

Every human being is born with the faculties of intuition and feeling connection. It is not bestowed upon some and denied others.

Does every human being know this? Possibly not!

Does every human being experience intuition? Yes, however for many, it may not be recognised as intuition.

It takes practice to develop and heighten your intuitive awareness. Even gifted intuitives practice. When I use the word practice I don't mean that it needs to be a deliberate, disciplined or rigid approach to practicing the craft of intuition, but it is about exercising the intuition muscle by tuning in and using it daily with an expectation of insights.

There are exercises included in this book to help you do this.

Being on a life path of self-understanding is integral to developing heightened intuition. Why? Because if you don't understand who you are first you won't have as much clarity around the insights and intuition you experience.

Skeptics

I expect you have heard there are left brain people (very analytical – need evidence and objective) and there are right brain people (intuitive, thoughtful and subjective).

Left brain people tend to be more skeptical about intuition because they want the evidence. This is why it can be important to locate the physical sensation that signals an intuitive insight.

Exercise: Discover Your Tangible Sign For Intuition

Some examples of a physical sensation or tangible sign are:
- goosebumps
- the hairs on the back of your neck stand up
- tingling in a certain part of your body
- a sensation in your solar plexus.

There are many more that are unique to individuals. The thing I ask you to do is to locate **your** physical sensation if you haven't done this already.

How do you locate your physical intuition signal?

Observe your body. Become conscious of the subtle things happening in or on your body and around you. Look for a signal that happens regularly. Once you recognise the signal, you'll know when your intuition is delivering you information.

You can either take note or ignore it – the choice is yours.

Practice Intuitive Exercises Daily

If you want to elevate your intuition you must practice. What I am talking about here is training in the same way you would train for the Olympics. If you want exceptional intuition, you have to put in the work. This is what I have done and my intuition is now finely attuned.

What sort of exercises will make a difference to your intuition? Perhaps they are different to what you would expect.

Exercise: Left Hand | Right Hand Drawing

You don't have to be an artist to draw like this. What this activity does is help you to express yourself, not necessarily create pictures that amaze and astound people.

It is important to get both sides of your brain talking to each other. One of the ways I've discovered is left and right hand drawing and writing.

Below is an overview of the exercise. If you would like to know more about this process I recommend you read this book - *The Power of Your Other Hand* by Lucia Capacchione.

I spent one year practicing the exercises in this book to help develop my intuition. One of the exercises is to draw a picture with your dominant hand and duplicate it with your non-dominant hand.

If you had asked me before I started if I could draw the answer would have been a big NO! And if you had asked if I could draw with my non-dominant hand it would have been an emphatic NO!

So what happened in this exercise?

It was a fun environment at the table with my kids, pencils, paper and a creative atmosphere. Drawing out of my head was not an option as I had never been able to do this, so I opened up one of the kids' Winnie the Pooh story books and thought I could possibly copy Owl.

It was surprising how easy it was to copy Owl with my dominant hand and then something amazing happened. When I put the pencil in my non-dominant hand and started copying Owl again a new dimension of clarity and confidence opened up. I discovered the artist within. Not only did I duplicate Owl with my non-dominant hand, but it looked and felt better than the first one.

There was a ripple effect from this one exercise (and Lucia Capacchione's book *The Power of Your Other Hand* is filled with many of these exercises). My confidence increased, especially when faced with a task that feels impossible or certainly is a challenge. Instead of saying, *"I can't do that!"* I now say, *"I'll give it a go!"*

Here are the drawings of Owl. I am right hand dominant.

8 Key qualities of intuitive insight

R- HAND   L- HAND

Which drawing do you like best?

Not only did I start drawing with both hands but I started writing with both hands. This is an extraordinary exercise for tapping into your subconscious and bringing the answers into the conscious domain that may otherwise remain hidden.

The process for tapping into your subconscious by writing with both hands is:

- Think of a question whilst holding a coloured felt pen in your dominant hand (the hand you normally write with).
- Write the question on a piece of paper.
- Hold a different coloured felt pen with your non-dominant hand and read the question again (either out loud or silently).
- Write the answer below the question.

This exercise works on many different levels and it is great to observe them all:

- You will notice that when the answer is more emotional it is more difficult to write legibly with your non-dominant hand.

- Your breathing will change rhythm when you are getting to the root of a problem. You may even develop a dry cough. This is a great signal to observe and use as a motivator to keep going.

- You may find when you are getting to the core of a problem you want to give up or distract yourself with an "urgent" task (this is called procrastination). Keep going as you'll appreciate the result.

- You may notice you think you know what you'll write with the non-dominant hand and the answer can be surprisingly different in a good way.

You may wonder what is the purpose of this exercise.

When you write or draw with your non-dominant hand the left brain or analytical aspect of self cannot make its presence felt. You are concentrating so intently on performing the next stroke of the pen, there is no space for the ego-mind chatter.

By doing this exercise you are building the bridge between your conscious and subconscious minds. This bridge is very helpful in triggering intuitive episodes.

Not only are you learning to tune into your subconscious mind, you are learning to tune into the collective consciousness where all answers reside.

When you practice this exercise you are 100% focused in the moment. And that is exactly what you want to be doing, training yourself to be 100% focused in the moment.

Being a person with an Olympian mindset didn't stop there. When Mum told me she used to write to a pen pal using the mirror writing technique I was intrigued and started doing it immediately.

Exercise: Mirror Writing

Mirror writing is when you start writing on the right hand side of the page and flip the letters backwards. When you hold the page up to a mirror you can read it as if you had written it from left to right). I started writing poetry in mirror writing. Here's an example of mirror writing.

This is an example of mirror writing.
This is an example of mirror writing.

The top line is written from right to left by flipping the letters around. The bottom line is what you see in the mirror.

Try it! You may find it becomes one of your fun activities.

In fact, I was so inspired by the feeling of clarity and insight this exercise created, I set myself a project and channeled 365 messages for a journal using the mirror writing technique. This journal will be published soon. Another one of my projects near completion.

Telephone | Email

Have you ever picked up your telephone for apparently no reason, put it back down and seconds later it rings? What just happened is you received the thoughts of the person calling you as they either entered your number on the keypad or they were searching for your number in their contacts list.

Have you ever heard your telephone ring and know who is calling you before you pick up the phone? This is for the same reason as above, you are receiving their thoughts about contacting you.

Exercise: Telepathy

You can grow this intuitive skill. Every time the phone rings tune into whom the caller may be. The secret for me is to reflect on the previous few minutes and recall who floated through my mind. The person ringing more often than not subtly touched my mind in that time with their thoughts.

This is a great exercise for becoming aware of the elusive and subtle connections that happen all the time as seemingly random thoughts. If you reach out to the people who touch your mind like this, you will get confirmation they were thinking of you.

Trust

Trust seems to be the most difficult quality to embrace when developing your intuition. This is why it is important to locate your tangible/physical sign of Truth.

At times, you'll find that the left-brain evidence indicates one thing, but your gut/intuition is saying another and you experience your tangible sign to confirm your intuition is correct. When this happens, trust your gut/intuition. Make a note of both choices. Choose which way you will go and then write the outcome next to the choice.

Keep a record of these experiences. I expect you will find the gut/intuitive response will have the best outcome.

A little experiment you can do is to ask your intuitive self which lane to drive in during heavy traffic. Despite the evidence – ie., one lane is moving faster than the other, listen to the little voice of intuition and move into the lane you intuit. Make a note of what happens. Invariably if I ignore my intuition I end up in the slow lane.

Note what happens?

You can also deliberately ignore the intuitive voice and note what happens. My experience has been frustration when I ignore the "VOICE"! However, it is good to do this side of the experiment as you gather proof of listening to and ignoring your intuition.

This is a great game to play to develop trust in your intuition. It's fun and doesn't feel like work.

The big question around this is *"What happens when you get the tangible sign, trust a choice and it turns out to be a terrible disaster?"*

My take on this is – when you release a goal, a wish, a desire to the Divine

8 Key qualities of intuitive insight

Being to manifest for you, you don't get to choose how that will be delivered to you and what skill set you need to embrace it.

Here's a story that illustrates this point very well.

My husband, Frank, was driving a taxi, we had two children in private schools and my health was fragile. We needed more money to make ends meet. When a friend told us about an opportunity to make the amount of money we needed, we thought our dreams were being answered. The tangible sign activated within me so we went ahead with our plans and handed over money we had borrowed.

Frank left his taxi job, so we only had my salary coming in. As it was a new opportunity, we weren't too concerned initially that the volume of work wasn't as much as expected. However, when the payments for our work began to run late we became worried.

It turned out to be an elaborate scam. We were luckier than most as we got our original investment back, only losing the taxi income for those weeks.

So what happened?? Did my intuition lead us up the garden path of failure?

NO!!

What happened was a miracle. Because of this seeming disaster, Frank was introduced to another taxi owner who gave him the opportunity to "single" a taxi 5 days a week for a set pay in. Singling is like leasing a taxi without the worry of repairs, maintenance and all the other legal and financial obligations. It also meant we had a second car during the week when we needed it.

Frank became one of the best taxi drivers in Brisbane and made more money doing this than he would have made if the business opportunity had turned out to be real.

Why have I told you this story? We had a goal of a certain amount of income each week and we put it out there to the Universe and didn't presume to know how it would arrive. By leaving the first taxi owner on the promise of more income, the way was opened up for a better opportunity that gave us two cars for 15 years – although we only paid the insurance, registration and maintenance for one. If we needed more money, Frank drove another hour or two.

When I got cancer some years after Frank started driving for this new taxi owner, he was given the taxi at no extra cost for another night to make life easier for me. This gift was priceless to us while I recovered. Interestingly, when my health returned, this gift continued for another 10 years.

So the message in this story is to look beyond a disaster to the opportunities it opens up for you. A disaster can give you a chance to dig deep into your internal reservoir, locate your inner strength and grow. This in turn will open you up to opportunities that may not have been possible before the perceived "disaster". God works in mysterious ways and my responsibility is to trust the flow and Divine Guidance.

How do you feel about this point? Take your time to really consider it.

What is Divine Guidance?

Divine Guidance is God connecting directly with you. It is knowledge, inner knowing, wisdom, and guidance that comes from the Divine Source or another term I use, the Divine Stream. The Divine Stream is within everyone. You can receive Divine Guidance.

Life changes remarkably when you tap into Divine Guidance. As I said above, Source knows the best route for you to follow and when you do, healing happens.

The challenge today for people is that they are disconnected from Divine Guidance and they don't know how to locate it. Their hearts are filled with fear, sorrow and/or anger, and the guidance can't shine its light through the thick resistance. When guidance does arrive, the ego-mind doubts it and takes no notice.

Divine Guidance comes through the purity of your heart. It comes from the place where you and the Divine Being are One. If you can locate that space and stay centered within it, the guidance comes easily and effortlessly to enrich and transform your life. This takes practice and discipline.

What's so special about Divine Guidance?

From my experience Divine Guidance brings you closer to Source.

Generally speaking, the world's focus on money, food and sex has taken people far away from their Divine roots. They've become trapped by their fear, sorrow and anger. To be truly happy the key is to reconnect with the Divine Source within and listen to the inner voice of Divine Guidance. This reconnects you with Source, Divine Being, God (use the words you are comfortable with).

Divine Guidance puts you in direct connection with the Divine voice. That voice is not outside of you – it is within you. It is within your heart, it's available and ready to give you all of the knowledge, direction, and support you need.

In conclusion, when you genuinely open up to Divine Guidance, it empowers you to be the best version of you possible. You have an inherent knowing of what to do, where to go and how to heal your inner and outer worlds.

Trust Your Insights, Intuition, Inner Knowing

Insights, intuition, inner knowing are all words to describe what can't be seen, but you know it as Truth at some level.

Interestingly, the single biggest comment I hear from people is *"I doubt my intuition!"*

Trust is a serious problem. Are you sitting there saying to yourself *"I know! Tell me about it!"*

I'd be lying if I said I didn't experience doubt, but I have learned to manage it.

The truth is when I schedule a new client I am invariably flooded with doubt and questions like:

- What if i get it completely wrong?
- What if i don't get anything?

The Art of Self-Healing

- What if i can't help this person?

go round in my mind.

However, every single time I work with someone – except on the very rare occasion when that person actually doesn't want the consultation and have come to please someone else – the accuracy is there and healing at an emotional, physical and spiritual level is achieved.

Is every session exceptional or extraordinary? This depends on how willing the client is to release their emotional blockages.

This is a key point for you to note when working with a therapist – the more willing and open you are to shift your blockages, the better the outcome.

It is important you trust the therapist to guide you through this process. If you don't trust the therapist, find another one. Don't keep spending money with someone you don't trust at a core level.

If my client doesn't trust me to facilitate their healing, I recommend they find another therapist. If they choose to find another therapist I understand it's not about me as a person, it simply means our energy signatures are not a match.

This way everyone stands in their integrity and maintains their authentic place in the world. The vibrational ripple effect of doing this has a direct and positive impact personally and on my business.

It is an amazing gift to self – to honour you and your boundaries.

How do you trust your insights, intuition and inner knowing? This comes with practice by looking for the tangible sign. The more familiar you become with the nuances and communication of your subtle bodies, the easier it is to trust your inner voice of knowing. Unfortunately, no one can give you this gift, you have to discover the process for yourself and then have the courage to take action based on your intuition.

Synchronicity and Serendipity

Earlier in the book, I talked about **synchronicity** (two or more events happening at the same time which are not causally related, but have meaning together) and **serendipity** (a pleasant unexpected happening). Here's the thing, these events are happening all the time, but you don't know unless you recognise them.

I live each day **expecting** to experience synchronicity and serendipity. Do you think I achieve my expectation? Yes, absolutely. Are they always profound and exceptional? No, but each day there is some evidence of synchronicity and serendipity.

However, I'm going to put a caveat on this; you can get addicted to looking for hidden meanings in everything that happens. This awareness of synchronicity and serendipity is not something that you can strategically initiate or control as much as you would like to and you probably will try to! But don't, it doesn't work! How do I know? I tried! **So here's a tip** – learn from my mistakes about this.

The secret to recognising synchronicity and serendipity is to simply observe life. Wonder or ponder in a curious way, not in a strategic way. When you get this subtle difference a whole new world will open up for you.

Again, this is not something anyone can teach you, it is something you have to discover for yourself.

Ethical

The dictionary states "ethical" as being in accordance with the rules or standards for **right conduct or practice**, especially the standards of a profession.

To put it bluntly, as an authentic human being hold yourself to the highest values. In my world this means:

- honesty
- do no harm

- no manipulation.

The more you explore your inner world and understand the possibilities of working with vibration, temptation to go over to the dark side becomes stronger. It is your responsibility to choose the light.

My son once said to me, *"It's easier to be in the dark!"* I agreed with him – it is easy to slide into the dark, it requires no effort or self-discipline, but it is not a good place to exist. I don't want to bring religion into this book, but for me living in the light = heaven and living in the dark = hell.

No one deserves to live in hell and everyone has the opportunity to live in heaven. It is a choice. God doesn't punish us, we punish ourselves.

And you can STOP IT!

The first step in healing is to stop punishing yourself.

Be Authentic

What do I mean by authentic? Simply put, discover who you are and live true to yourself? Or in other words – walk your talk.

Do you know your core values? The following activity can help you to find out what your core values are. (Hoople, 2012)

Exercise: Find Your Core Values

- Write down 20 values that really resonate with you.
- Narrow down those 20 values to the 10 most important.
- Narrow down those 10 values to the 5 most important.
- Decide their order of importance. Determine which of the 5 is least important, which is most important.
- Do some creative journaling/brainstorming with your 5 most important core values. Write down and possibly illustrate what each of those values means to you. "Beauty" might mean:
    - having an attractive personal appearance to one person

- surrounding oneself with beauty to another
- maybe creating beauty to someone else
- or it might mean all of the above
• Return to your list of core values whenever you're making a decision. Ask yourself: *"Is this in line with my 5 most important values?"*

The thing is that when you live by your core values, people can feel this and they trust you at a deep level without even understanding why. We communicate in many different ways – speech, facial expression, body language, thoughts, feelings, belief systems – you can feel all of these about another person.

So my question to you is ***"Do you live by your core values?"***

If your answer is yes – awesome! Keep it up!

If your answer is no – then you can start today! It's never too late to start.

When you live your life by your core values your passion and purpose illuminates you from within. Your body moves in flow, you glow with vitality and your wisdom is clear for all to see, feel and hear.

Be Real

What do I mean by "be real"? In this instance, it means be genuine, be who you are warts and all. By being the real you will attract people who resonate with you and your inherent qualities.

Will these qualities be for everyone? Absolutely not! For example, if you are an idealist, it is likely a realist would not be attracted to your energy signature nor would they want to hang out with you unless there is an area of resonance between you.

I'm an idealist! Has this caused me problems – YES, but that's okay. I smile now rather than feel wounded and misunderstood.

Are you an idealist or a realist? Here's some help if you are not sure.

An idealist has some or many of these qualities:

The Art of Self-Healing

- **Dreamer** – a person whose ideas or projects are considered audacious or highly speculative.
- **Enthusiast** – a person filled with or motivated by enthusiasm.
- **Escapist** – an inclination to or habit of retreating from unpleasant or unacceptable reality through diversion or fantasy.
- **Optimist** – the tendency to expect the best and see the best in all things.
- **Radical** – a person who favours extreme or fundamental change in existing institutions or in political, social, or economic conditions.
- **Romanticist** – someone who indulges in excessive sentimentality.
- **Seer** – a person endowed with profound moral and spiritual insight or knowledge; a wise person or sage who possesses intuitive powers.
- **Theorizer** – a person who creates theories.
- **Transcendentalist** – a person who follows the philosophy of transcendentalism. It calls on people to view the objects in the world as small versions of the whole universe and to trust their individual intuitions.
- **Utopian** – of or relating to a perfect or ideal existence.
- **Visionary** – characterized by idealistic or radical ideas, esp impractical ones (*My view on this description is – where would the world be today without the visionaries! These people are our pioneers who make discoveries realists say are impossible.*).

A realist (or rationalist) is someone who emphasizes observable facts and excludes metaphysical speculation about origins or ultimate causes.

A realist has some or many of these qualities:

- **Analytical** – capable of or given to analysing.
- **Deductive reasoning** – is a logical process in which a conclusion is made from a set of premises and contains no more information than

those premises.

- **Logical** – capable of or characterized by clear or valid reasoning.
- **Objective** – not influenced by personal feelings, interpretations, or prejudice; based on facts; unbiased.
- **Reasoning** – the process of forming conclusions, judgments, or inferences from facts or premises.
- **Reflective** – characterized by quiet thought or contemplation.
- **Sensible** – having or showing good sense or judgment.
- **Thoughtful** – showing careful thought and consideration.

A succinct way of describing the differences between them would be that idealism is "what could be" where realism is "what actually is".

Let's consider life as a cut diamond with many facets – when you have balance in your life you see all the facets on the diamond. If you are more idealistic and less objective, you may take more risks when making your decisions. If you are more of a realist, you may miss out on positive opportunities because the facts don't stack up in an objective way.

To create balance for your decision making as an idealist or a realist, consciously introduce the qualities you are not strong in and practice using them when making your decisions in a more rounded way.

For example: as an idealist, I practice gathering all the facts to support my intuitive, metaphysical decision. Do I manage this all the time, no, but it is a discipline I work on embracing.

I encourage you to balance out your decision making process so that you feel more informed and empowered when you make your choices.

Chapter Notes

Chapter 10
The Rules of Vibrational Healing?

I understand that you may want to experiment with friends and family with the things you are learning in this book. And that is great. However, there are some rules to be mindful of when using psychic medicine or intuitive healing practices on others?

These are the rules given to me in 1984 and I have abided by them since that time. You may or may not agree with these rules and you must choose whether to follow them or not. However, they are the rules I was given – and have written them accordingly.

Rule #1 – Always Ask Permission

The first RULE when doing energy work is to be given permission to enter a person's energy body.

VERY IMPORTANT: Do not decide for yourself because someone looks sick, or is sick and could or would benefit from your help that you have permission to initiate psychic medicine or intuitive healing on them. This is an invasion of their personal space and privacy.

Imagine if someone did that to you and you didn't want someone messing with your energy body. Most likely you wouldn't appreciate it – and I suspect you would prefer to be asked so you could have the opportunity of saying no if you want to. And I have had people say no – so be respectful.

People are where they are in their life because of choices. Sometimes good choices and sometimes seemingly poor choices, but nevertheless their choices. At other times "things" happen that make people wonder whether they "had done some terrible things" in another life because this life is so tough and ask whether there is anymore that has to be endured.

There are no simple answers to this question. However, what I am clear about is that everyone is responsible for their bodies and that means all of them – the physical, emotional, mental and spiritual bodies as well as the esoteric – auric, energy and etheric bodies.

If a person needs help with their health as is often the case, it is each person's responsibility to ask for that help. In my experience, the asking is part of the healing process.

It is reasonable for you to offer your help, but don't presume permission is given and if you do ask, you may be surprised how often you will be given a "no thank you, but thank you for asking" response.

REMEMBER: For someone to allow you to enter their energy field is a huge act of trust. And everyone's energy is not compatible. So a great level of respect needs to be present when doing psychic medicine or intuitive healing. Honour a person's desire to protect their energy.

To be told NO can sometimes feel like a slap in the face. Especially when you know you can help. Nevertheless, it is not about you, it's about what feels intuitively right for each individual. And everything is in Divine timing – not your timing.

Why This Rule?

I would be guessing if I answered this question. However, the fact is it was given to me as a direct, undeniable instruction at the beginning of my metaphysical and intuitive awakening. I have honoured this instruction to this day. It hasn't been easy. I've been painfully tested at times, as you will be too if you decide to explore this path.

A Coma Patient

I remember being asked to work with a man in a coma. Clearly, a coma patient cannot give permission for psychic medicine to be done. As much as I wanted to break this rule, my commitment to honour it was stronger than my compassion for his wife's terrible predicament – which was tremendously strong.

I know this man's wife was deeply wounded by my rejection of her request to scan his body and help him as she thought I was her last hope.

Rule #2 – Protect Your Energy

Here is a lesson I learned the hard way. If you start working with other people doing energy healing work, without proper protection and strong personal boundaries you may well experience a decline in your health. I didn't understand this for a long time.

My limiting belief was that I had to survive cancer to be an authentic medical intuitive. Yes, I have survived cancer, but I didn't need to do that to be validated in this field. If I had protected my energy in a disciplined manner, looked after my energy body better, managed my emotions better perhaps I could have avoided cancer.

A wise person learns from the mistakes of others.

A significant contributing factor to becoming ill is poor energy protection. Please be disciplined about protecting your energy when doing this kind of work. It is also important to protect the energy of the person you are working with, too.

Prayer of Protection

Here is my Prayer of Protection again:
"In the name of Jesus Christ, I call upon the spirits of light who stand guard at the doorway of my soul to guide me in the ways of truth, love and light ... and protect me from the forces of darkness and deception. Amen"

Rev. Marilyn O'Sullivan of the Spiritualist Church in Brisbane taught this prayer to her psychic development students. I took her 8 week psychic development class and it is part of my daily life.

Use this prayer or design your own. However, do use a prayer of protection when doing psychic/intuitive or inter-dimensional work.

Before I enter the energy body of my client, I instinctively say this prayer.

Template: Tongue To The Roof Of The Mouth

This template is one of the best I have experienced for protecting your energy. It's not just for people working in the intuitive or psychic area. Go to page 26 for the instructions.

Template: Tips of Fingers Together

You may have noticed public speakers and people who are being interviewed place the tips of their fingers together as if they are wrapping their hands around a softball.

This, too, is a technique for closing your energy circuits. It is a way of protecting your energy from being drained and keeps your energy strong.

This technique is well worth remembering.

The thing with both the **tip of the tongue** and the **tips of fingers together** is they are strategies you can do and no one need know you are doing them [except the people who know the technique, too].

Not only are they effective when you are doing intuitive medicine or psychic work, but you can use them in all areas of your life. Particularly with those friends and family who drain you.

Yes, they will feel great after spending time with you and you feel like a wrung out dish rag. It's time to stop this and protect your energy by using either of the above methods.

Rule #3 - Cleanse Your Energy

Template: Hold Hands Under Running Water

I'm not sure where I learned this energy cleansing strategy, but it has proved to be invaluable.

Hold your hands under cool running water for a couple of minutes and consciously ask that your energy body be cleared of all vibration that is not for your highest good. This is particularly important when you are doing hands on energy work.

However, I find this ritual very beneficial after all psychic or intuitive contact.

You can also use the templates in Chapter 1.

Template: Cut Energy Cords

When you connect intuitively, energetically or psychically with someone you create a strong energy bond. This bond is a deeper connection than every day interactions with others.

I refer to these bonds as psychic cords and if you do not deliberately cut these psychic cords, you are bound to that person in a way that can establish a psychic drain on your energy. Without proper management, the energy needs of the person you work with will determine how much of a drain they are on you.

If the person you connect with is sick, they are energetically seeking any means of re-energising themselves they can. Energy cords are one of the first

The Art of Self-Healing

ways they do this.

In saying that it sounds like this is a malicious and reprehensible act. Most of the time this is done unconsciously and is a primal act of survival. Most people would be mortified to know they are doing it.

With you being responsible and deliberately cutting these cords after every psychic/intuitive connection, your energy levels will stay stronger.

I strongly recommend you cut all energy cords daily whether they are made from psychic/intuitive connections or standing next to someone in the street. Make it a practice to cut all cords daily.

I hear you saying *"I don't have time!"*

That's not true!

When you go to bed at night make it the last thing you do before falling to sleep. You can do it in 1-2 minutes. See Personal Cleansing template on page 18.

If you have any other rituals or practices when doing healing on others – then continue with them. If you don't already observe the rules above, consider including them.

You don't HAVE to follow these rules; however they have helped me develop exceptional intuitive skills since 1984.

Chapter 11
Where does Illness or Disease Begin?

The question *"Where does illness or disease begin?"* has been the core of my research and development for 30 years.

In this lifetime, the body known as Julie Lewin has experienced much illness, disease and pain. There have been 6 major surgeries and multiple minor procedures to remove diseased body parts and growths including cancer.

When I was told at the age of 25 I could see inside of people's bodies (and should I choose to use this gift would be of great benefit to mankind) I had a thought. I had decided that to be recognised as a true healer and someone who could speak with authority, I had to survive cancer. This thought stayed with me over the years.

When I was diagnosed with thyroid cancer, the specialist said to me, *"If you are going to get cancer, this is the best one to get as we can treat it quite successfully"*. It was a small comfort to hear this. Thankfully I survived the cancer and can

The Art of Self-Healing

now share my life's work with you.

People often ask why I experienced so much illness and disease.

Firstly, it has rewarded me with tremendous insight into the illness and discomfort of others. When you personally experience symptoms of illness or disease, it is incredible how comforting it is to talk with someone who has a true understanding of what you are going through. It is also inspiring to speak to someone who has recovered and is living a healthy life.

In this respect, I feel blessed to have been gifted with this depth of recognition and level of empathy for the people I help through their suffering.

Secondly, my conclusion about the question **"What is the root cause of illness and disease?"** is that illness and disease is the result of chronic trapped, suppressed and unresolved emotion. And this can be from this lifetime or previous lifetime(s).

My story

At 40, I was diagnosed with 4 thyroid diseases: cancer, multi-nodular goitre, Plummer's Disease (toxic nodule/s that produce too much thyroid hormone (hyperthyroidism)) and Hashimoto's Disease (an autoimmune disease causing hypothyroidism (underactive thyroid)).

At this point in my life, I was passively seeking death. To function each day was a huge struggle. After learning about the thyroid and understanding its vital role in health and well-being, I suspect I suffered from undiagnosed thyroid imbalance from my first pregnancy in 1984. This diagnosis explained my daily struggle to function, living with 4 thyroid diseases culminating in thyroid cancer in 2000.

The question is why did the imbalance happen in the first place?

This is where my research gets interesting. The thyroid is located in the throat at the throat chakra which is the seat of communication. Until I was diagnosed with thyroid cancer, I avoided conflict. I wanted to be liked and needed. I didn't have a strong opinion. I felt invisible. I pushed my thoughts, wants and desires down in an attempt to keep peace and harmony in all areas of my life.

Did this work for me and for those around me?

NO!!! It led to deep seated frustration and resentment and finally apathy for the physical world on my part.

I annoyed the people in my life because I wouldn't communicate for fear of upsetting them.

The more these emotions filled my body, the more "I" left my body for other dimensions. This was awesome in one way as I became very proficient at inter-dimensional travel and developed my metaphysical abilities to an exceptional level.

However, my understanding is this – we are born into the physical dimension to experience it fully. At the end of 2001, I realised my purpose was to be fully present in my body and integrate the extraordinary metaphysical and spiritual lessons and observations I had experienced into an ordinary life.

This has not been an easy process after a lifetime of skipping out. However, with each year that passes, I am more successful at being fully present in my body.

How do I know this mission has been successful? As each year passes, my body achieves a better level of health and wellbeing. My bowel has stopped growing tumours; my breasts are lump free; the relapse in thyroid cancer has been transformed without medical intervention and my level of health and wellness is the best ever.

I have been discharged from the cancer clinic in full remission and my doctor of 20 years says she hasn't seen me look so well as now.

Since we left the city and moved to the country in 2010, we live a less stressful life, drink rain water (no fluoride present), grow and eat organic vegetables straight from the garden and eat our own organic, free range eggs. Being healthy under these conditions has been easier to achieve.

I have learned to speak my truth under most circumstances, and if I don't do this my body tells me very quickly and this is a great prompt to smarten up and communicate authentically.

Emotion influences our beliefs which triggers a vibration. This impacts our cells which in turn creates the healthy or unhealthy structure of our body.

What about babies born with disease or deformity?

I can't definitively answer this question – however, my belief is this – the "I" we refer to when describing who we are does not refer to the body, more to the soul, and that "I" does not die. I believe the body drops and the "I" continues to grow and evolve wherever the "I" consciousness travels to when it leaves the body.

We don't really know what happens to the soul, although the work of Michael Newton in *"Journey of Souls"* is an amazing account of life after death which I encourage you to read. This book had a powerful influence on how I perceive death and what happens to the soul between lives.

These are some things I've learned as an adult in relation to this.

- We do not know God's plan – for ourselves or for others.
- We do not know what agreements a soul makes before returning to the physical form.
- We do not know why one is afflicted and another isn't.

I am, however, confident in saying that emotion is the root cause of discomfort, illness and disease, whether that is emotion from this lifetime or emotion trapped in the soul from previous lifetimes.

Trapped or unresolved emotion initially affects the esoteric bodies creating holes in the aura and weakening them. When trapped energy builds up in one place (you will notice this through extra heat in certain areas of the body) it will ultimately become denser and affect your physical body. It is best to release this heat as soon as possible. There are a number of ways you can do this.

Here are some methods:

Where does illness or disease begin

1. Acupuncture
2. A variety of Emotional Release Techniques
3. Hypnosis
4. Neuro Linguistic Programming (NLP)
5. Hands on healing
6. The Art of Self-Healing (using an advanced template I've developed)

Emotions

One day I began thinking about the 3 primary colours – red, yellow and blue. I wondered, if there are 3 primary colours, are there 3 primary emotions? And if there are 3 primary emotions, would it be possible to simply work with those emotions and dissolve all the sub-emotions in the process?

Have you ever experienced an answer dropping into your mind?

That's literally what happened next. These words touched my mind – *"I was so angry I saw red!"* – AAAhhhh, so ANGER is a primary emotion and relates to the primary colour RED.

Then the words – *"I am feeling blue today!"* touched my mind. This saying means I feel sad so another primary emotion is SORROW and it relates to the primary colour BLUE.

Wondering what the third primary emotion could be – these words flashed through my mind *"He's yellow – he ran away!"* It came with a vision of a soldier running away from the frontline. I knew immediately that the third primary emotion is FEAR and it relates to the last primary colour – YELLOW.

Here's how the primary emotions are broken down:

- **FEAR** – anxiety, terror, phobias, overwhelm
- **SORROW** – melancholy, depression, grief, sadness
- **ANGER** – frustration, jealousy, revenge, rage

These emotions can be broken down further eg., jealousy => envy, dissatisfaction, rivalry and you can go on refining the specific emotion.

But ultimately – all emotion comes back to these 3 primary emotions.

My premise is if you balance the 3 primary emotions, you potentially can balance all the emotions.

Balance your tangible emotions in 5 minutes

Now you'll notice I used the words **tangible emotions**. By this I mean the emotions you are experiencing right now, as opposed to the emotions that are trapped or blocked in your energy and physical body over time. Before we discuss this, I want to share with you a simple breathing technique to balance emotions.

Often it is difficult to identify the emotion you are experiencing. It could be a mixture of emotions and you don't know which one is more dominant. If you can't identify your primary emotion, this process will help you.

Start by asking yourself *"What colour am I relating to – red, blue or yellow?"*

Rather than trying to identify and name your feeling use the colour to give you an insight into your root emotion. Sometimes you will be feeling different emotions at the same time, but one will be the root or primary emotion. This is the one to balance first.

Another clue to understanding your primary emotion at any given time is simply to observe your breath (during normal activities – not during or just after playing sport, running or doing strenuous work). When you observe your breath, if you are experiencing:

- **Fear** – you'll notice a shallow breath in and out;
- **Sorrow** – you'll notice a long, hard, fast, breath in, and a short shallow breath out (you may also observe involuntarily sighs);
- **Anger** – you'll notice a short shallow breath in, but a long, hard, fast breath out.

Keep a journal of your observations about your emotions for at least a week before beginning the following breathing technique. This way you'll become familiar with the different nuances of your breathing.

Exercise: Balance Emotions With the Breath

- To perform this simple technique it's best to be sitting comfortably either in a meditation pose or on a chair with your feet flat on the floor.
- Become conscious of your breath. Focus on a point at the front of your nose and your top lip.
- While doing this:-
  - to the count of 10, breathe steadily in filling your entire lungs; and
  - to the count of 10, steadily release the breath all the way out, completely emptying your lungs
- Continue this process for 5 minutes.
- This simple breathing technique will balance your emotions. With practice, you will manage out of control emotional outbursts calmly, and effectively deal with day to day challenges.
- By practicing this technique each day for five minutes you will transform every area of your life for the better.

Inner Conflict

Inner conflict is a key trigger of illness and disease. It is the private battle that goes on within you. It could be about anything from choosing between two job offers, to making all sorts of decisions in your personal and public life.

I'm telling you about this battle that occurs for two reasons:

(a) as you develop your intuitive skills you will experience this phenomenon frequently. You will second guess yourself and discount what you intuit; and

(b) your family and friends will experience it and by learning the signs and symptoms of inner conflict, you are better able to help if the opportunity arises and you are invited to help.

My experience has been that the first thing you intuit is accurate, and more specifically when you get your tangible signal at the same time (such as goosebumps or tingles) this will confirm your intuition.

The other factor that causes inner conflict is the actual information you intuit. When receiving intuitive messages, particularly about the health of others, if you are not a health practitioner, it is not your responsibility to name the problem, but rather to guide that person to seek help from a health professional, whether that be allopathic or alternative.

As I was learning about the subtleties of using my intuition, I made mistakes.

One day I rang Mum, excited to share my insight about a future happening involving Dad. I said, *"Dad is going to get sick and you are going to worry he will die, but he won't die. Isn't that great news!"*

I didn't consider how this would impact Mum. I was thinking only that it was great he wouldn't die and wanted to give her this encouragement before the event.

A couple of weeks later Dad had a biopsy and he got a blood infection making him very ill. Mum did worry he would die. Thankfully, he pulled through.

Afterwards, she asked me to keep any future insights to myself. She didn't want to know and I agreed not to share.

Some years later, Dad asked me to check inside and tell him what was happening as he wasn't feeling well. I performed my scan and discovered he had lung cancer.

Being mindful of Mum's request, I told him to ask his doctor for a chest x-ray. His doctor ordered an endoscopy (a camera down the oesophagus into the stomach). I repeated my request, *"Dad, you need to have a chest x-ray"* and he did.

Where does illness or disease begin

The x-ray showed a mass in his lung which turned out to be lung cancer. He had surgery to remove the cancer. Unfortunately, he developed post-op complications and he passed peacefully a few days later.

I am glad I didn't share my insight with Dad. Although, he may have suspected he had cancer, he didn't know for sure until after the surgery and just before he died. As a family, we didn't have a drawn out experience of watching him deteriorate and die and for that we are grateful.

If you are experiencing inner conflict in your life this can most definitely affect your energy bodies and if not resolved, ultimately it will become denser and trigger physical disease.

I learned through painful experience that inner conflict causes disease and illness. Yet even with all I have learned over 30 years, I still create anomalies in my wellbeing.

It is a reminder to be vigilant with my thoughts and to process emotions consciously and regularly.

Process Emotions

There are many ways to process emotions. Here are several ways:

1. Write a letter.
2. Keep an emotion journal – Mari L. McCarthy is the Goddess of journaling – www.createwritenow.com.
3. Talk to a confidante you trust.
4. Work with a therapist skilled in releasing emotional build up.

Exercise: Write a letter

This is an incredibly powerful exercise which I feel is a forgotten healing art. Write a letter to the person whose words or actions have initiated your emotional turmoil. Let it all flow out of you as fast as you can write it.

NOTE: Handwrite the letter rather than type it because handwriting accesses a different part of your brain and you connect with your emotions better. It may take longer to write, but it is worth it. Make the letter as long as there is flow; keep writing until there is no residue of emotion left around this situation. The true blessing from this process is to end the letter with your learnings.

NO! You are not going to post it, as much as you may want to. Instead you are going to have a burning ceremony. This is a powerful emotional cleanse.

Build a small fire, either inside or outside and make a ceremony out of the process. You can have candles, incense, singing bowl, bells or gong or anything you have on hand. Have a pre-written prayer or allow free thought to flow through you as you set the intention to release all the emotion to the universe.

This is a sacred act for you, not a punishing act about or against another. You are doing this to be relieved of destructive trapped emotion that will not serve your holistic wellbeing.

Exercise: Keep an emotion journal

I've kept journals on and off for most of my adult life. Sometimes I re-read them, other times I don't. The important thing is to reflect. I like to write down what I've learned. Sometimes I discover things about myself I don't like and other times I'm grateful, proud and in awe of the process of self-understanding.

Mari McCarthy from www.createwritenow.com has everything you need to journal effectively. Mari generously offers a bonus for you on her website.

Exercise: Have a confidante

The meaning of confidante is *a person to whom secrets are confided or with whom private matters and problems are discussed.*

My experience with a confidante is that they listen, ask probing questions, but **do not** try to fix your problem. When you have a true confidante to discuss your problems with, this will assist you to unravel the trapped emotions caught up in the drama of what's happening.

We all have the solution to our problems, we just need the space to verbalise

Where does illness or disease begin

and work through it. My Mum helps me with this.

I am not saying here that you go and verbally vomit all over someone and walk away feeling better. If you do this you won't have a friend/confidante for very long and also you run a high risk of initiating a tight downward spiral of emotion that sucks both of you into the whirlpool. No benefit is gained for you and you've contaminated your friend/confidante as well.

A great confidante is someone who doesn't mix with you socially. They don't know the people or situations about which you are emotionally processing.

The risk you run of choosing a confidante who is involved in your social scene, work environment or knows the people or situations you are processing is that they will betray your confidence.

The key to any communication with a confidante is to have the **purpose** of self-understanding from every connection with them.

Always set the intention to discover the higher learning from your experiences as this helps you grow your self-understanding at a great speed. You receive gifts in every encounter and you release trapped emotion before it manifests as a tangible illness or disease.

Trauma

Physical trauma is defined as *a body wound or shock produced by sudden physical injury, as from violence or accident.* Mental trauma is defined as *an experience that produces psychological injury or pain.*

All trauma carries an emotional signature and can be the root cause of illness and disease. The shock of trauma triggers the emotion to penetrate deep into the fabric of the body/mind.

This emotion can become locked with a blanket of amnesia around it and the incident is seemingly forgotten in the memories. However, our cells remember and hold the vibration of the trauma long after the wounds have physically and mentally healed.

An interesting phenomenon I've discovered is that when trauma occurs not only is the emotion of the incident locked in, but the emotion of the day-to-day life at that time is also locked in.

So what can you do about this?

Brandon Bays has done extensive work on releasing trauma from the cells. She has called this body of work "Journeying" and has written an international best seller called "The Journey". Brandon's work has helped many thousands of people around the world heal their body/mind and if you are drawn to this style of work, I encourage you to explore it.

I have deliberately not studied Brandon's work as I feel the work I am guided to do is to remain founded in intuition rather than in a set process such as Journeying.

Beliefs – where do they come from?

Every moment billions of events are happening and it is impossible to absorb and process the meaning of all of those events. You filter them according to their importance in your life and the way you filter these events is through your belief system.

Your belief system is cultivated from the moment you are born. It is influenced by your parents, grandparents, nannies, siblings, teachers, friends, heroes, TV shows, music, books, travel, church, and even the websites you visit. They all influence the way you think and how you behave.

Your belief system is also shaped by what happens to you. Sometimes this happens consciously through personal development and self-understanding, but more often than not your beliefs are being developed subconsciously.

A great way of knowing what has influenced your belief system is to keep a journal.

Often I have re-read my journals and discover where my beliefs actually originate from. It is fascinating to locate the root of a belief.

Your beliefs go on to form subconscious patterns which determine how you respond to life's dance. One response feels perfectly natural to you yet can seem quite bizarre to another.

If you want to be well physically, mentally, emotionally and spiritually learn to understand your patterns. When you recognise a pattern that is not supporting you, the best choice for you is to let it fall away.

Sound hard??? Or Easy???

In my experience it can be both. It depends on how much emotion is tied up in the pattern.

The interesting thing about "Lessons" is they begin quite mildly – almost like a mild curry – sometimes you don't even notice it is a curry (the lesson). The next time the lesson comes around there seems to be a bit more curry and you certainly know it is a curry, but it's not too hot, and you can tolerate the consequences.

So the story goes on and each time the lesson gets more heat (if we continue with the curry analogy) or more magnified and outrageous until it is very clear what the pattern is and that you should just STOP IT!!!!

This can be easier said than done and I stick my hand up in acknowledgement of this. However, when I learned the process of observing my behaviour **objectively** rather than **subjectively**, the patterns become easier to identify. It now becomes an informed choice I make whether I continue with the pattern or stop.

To observe objectively is to be free of the influence of personal feelings, interpretations or prejudice. You simply look at the facts. In other words, observe without your belief filters.

To observe subjectively is to be in the mind with all your belief filters creating interpretations and giving significance beyond the facts. Subjective observation includes the myriad of emotions you experience which colours your world and hides your patterns.

Journaling is one of the best ways to see your patterns. If you haven't done this before, you will need to be persistent and practice. It's just like any new skill you need to practice to get comfortable with it and then more practice to become confident.

It's not necessary, but I find it is part of the sacred ritual to use a nice journal that feels special to touch as you enter a sacred sanctuary when you take time to write your observations from the day. It doesn't need to be a long process. The discipline of writing your objective observations and learning from the day is the key.

There is a huge difference between a conscious pattern and a subconscious pattern.

When you are aware of a conscious pattern in action ie., you are deliberately behaving in a particular way to get a certain outcome, the complication of emotional filters is not present. In other words, the reactive cycle is being controlled by one party, you.

If the reactive cycle changes in the interaction and emotions are reactive by all parties, it has slipped across the invisible barrier into a subconscious pattern.

Conscious or subconscious patterns don't equal right or wrong, the pattern "just is". However, when you understand your patterns you can choose to let the ones not serving you go and consciously embrace the patterns that do serve you.

I use the word "serve" in the context that it helps you live to your highest potential.

Vibrational Impact on Health

The number 7 has significantly shaped my belief system. We know there are 7 major chakra centers[1] in the body.

- Root chakra – Muladhara – RED
- Sacral chakra – Swadhisthana – ORANGE
- Solar plexus chakra – Manipura – YELLOW
- Heart chakra – Anahata – GREEN
- Throat chakra – Vishuddha – BLUE

- Brow (third eye) chakra – Ajna – PURPLE
- Crown chakra – Sahasrara – VIOLET

I propose there are 7 bodies that correlate to the chakra colours and collectively make up our whole being. They are:

- Physical body - RED
- Emotional body - ORANGE
- Mental body - YELLOW
- Auric body - GREEN
- Energy body - BLUE
- Spiritual body - PURPLE
- Etheric body - VIOLET

Beginning with the solid physical body, these bodies become more subtle till you reach the etheric body.

Every interaction or awareness you have creates a tangible frequency between you and a person or thing. It sometimes can be seen via the third eye as a thread with a hook on either end connecting you with that experience or person. This thread will hook into any of your bodies depending on its vibration and will connect with any part of your body.

If these hooks are not consciously dissolved, released, cut, burned, pulled out (the process of releasing them is as creative as your imagination) they build up over time, become more solid and ultimately manifest as disease or illness in the physical and mental bodies.

I didn't understand this principle until one day I couldn't function any more. As my intuitive skills developed, I ignorantly made many miss-takes. These miss-takes shaped who I am today. I made them because I wanted to understand WHY and discover what I could do differently. Many of these insights were without guidance from a living mentor, but came through observation, inspection and Divine Guidance. I had visions which I wondered about and pondered on.

Template: Regeneration meditation

One of these visions was observing my body walking along a dirt track in the bush. There was grass growing between the wheel tracks. From my observation point, I could see ribbons, threads, trees and cables that were attached to my body floating out of my vision to whomever they were connected to.

It was not relevant to me who the connections were with. I felt inspired to cut, burn, disconnect, or pull them all out. The interesting thing that happened here was that as I continued to walk along the path the body became more subtle, and I could see the more subtle connections to this body. So they were removed and the body became more subtle revealing the more subtle connections.

Once I had observed the seven bodies releasing these connections a faint outline of light remained in my vision. The dissociation with these bodies ended and the separate observer "I" re-merged with the light body and I was pulled into a tremendous bright tunnel of light.

In this bright light, there was no perception of being solid or separate. I later learned this bright light is the Chamber of Rejuvenation. I couldn't tell you the length of human time that "I" stayed in this chamber, but there was an awareness of my physical body gradually feeling strengthened and restored energetically.

There came a point where it felt time to move through to the other side of the chamber. I stepped through an invisible wall. From one moment to the next I went from bright Light into an incredible green field with a gentle rise to the right.

I felt compelled to lie down on the grass. As I lay there I felt plugged into the core of the Earth feeling her vitality surge through me. I had an awareness of my whole being regenerating. My inner reservoir refilled as a tangible experience.

Where does illness or disease begin

When I came out of this journey my physical wellbeing had been restored and I was able to function again. At the time, I didn't understand the implication of this process and didn't repeat it. Unfortunately, my health deteriorated and I found myself utterly exhausted again. I remembered this vision and repeated the process again with great results but the exhaustion continued to reoccur.

Sometimes I am a slow learner, but eventually I realised the experience I had with the subtle bodies, the Chamber of Rejuvenation and the Field of Regeneration must be a daily discipline. It helps keep your physical and subtle bodies clear of connection overload. You sleep more deeply and wake feeling refreshed and rejuvenated. Listen to Insight Timer insig.ht/gm_1270

Weakness In Your Energy Bodies

The key to having a healthy physical body is to have healthy subtle bodies. The way to do this is through creative and spontaneous visualisation. The vision I shared with you above is the sort of visualisation I mean here.

Have you ever wondered how someone can walk out of a total car wreck with little or no damage to their body? Ever wondered why someone dies in a car accident and there doesn't seem to be much damage to the car or their body?

I wondered this for a long time. The conclusion I came to is that the state of the subtle bodies determines what impact the accident has on the physical body.

When I was 5 months pregnant with our daughter someone told me a story of a man who was speared through the head while driving his car. Tragically, something had dislodged from a moving vehicle in front and turned into a missile. There was no damage to the car except where the object penetrated the windscreen. The man died.

I was shocked to hear of this freak accident and it stayed in my mind when I was driving. Would you believe within weeks of hearing this story, I was driving along the dual highway at 100km/hour and I saw movement in the back of a truck in front of me. Can you imagine my surprise and horror as I saw an object spinning through the air like a missile coming straight for my head?

I hadn't been checking my mirrors so didn't know if there was a car in the lane next to me. I took my hands off the steering wheel, wrapped them around my abdomen and crouched forward behind the steering wheel as far as possible to avoid being injured by the unidentified missile.

You hear people talk about everything happening in slow motion and for me this was one of those moments. The object hit the metal strip where the windscreen met the roof of the car, cracked the windscreen and gauged a hole about 10cm into the roof.

I sat up immediately after impact and watched where the object landed in my mirror and pulled over to the side of the road before shock set in.

Did the story about the man dying prepare me for this experience? Did this knowledge somehow strengthen my energy body?

There is no way of knowing for sure, but I do believe this – the angels, God (whoever or whatever you want to name it) assisted me that day with strengthening my energy body and a tragedy was avoided.

Could the energy body have created a force field deflecting the object from penetrating the car? We'll never know. There are some incredible and extraordinary stories to be told and I just wonder what really happens in these situations when you consider the power of the energy bodies together with the physical body.

So what does this all mean? You'll need to work out for yourself what it means to you, but for me it means that our emotions, connections, experiences, belief systems and our patterns impact on all of our bodies.

It can be inspirational and uplifting in a way that has the energy centers vibrating at optimum levels and your physical body function is vital and healthy or it can impact the body in a degenerating downward spiral creating illness and disease.

Cells

Let's move deeper into the physical body.

The mystery of conception and a new life being created from 2 cells coming together has fascinated me forever. The DNA computer which regulates our growth, cell division, puberty and menopause is quite mind boggling when you really consider it.

In David Wilcock's book *The Hidden Science of Lost Civilisations* he provides scientific evidence for the multi-dimensional research I've been doing since 1984.

The following paragraph excited me, *"We know that many illnesses are enhanced or even caused by stress – and it could be that when we get stressed out or go through negative emotions, we're giving away some of our own vitality by shedding the light stored in our DNA, all throughout our cells ... Therefore in order to get healthy again, we're going to have to charge our DNA back up – and get more light."*

These words validated evidence I had discovered in my work.

Some more exciting research mentioned by David Wilcock was the work of Fritz-Albert Popp, a theoretical biophysicist at the University of Marburg in Germany. Popp learned that many biological lab experiments have proven you can destroy 99 percent of a cell with ultraviolet light, but if you then give it a very weak pulse of the same wavelength, it almost completely recovers – in a single day. This is known as "photo repair" and the best photo repair effects are known to occur at 380 nanometres. [2]

There is more interesting research in David's book, but in the context of what I want to share with you now I don't need to include that information here. However, if you are interested in the scientific evidence of quantum physics, I recommend you read this book with a highlighter pen!

What I'm about to share with you now is the structure of how my work has unfolded since 1984.

I hear, read or learn about a concept, an idea, or in this case research and I use that information to create a healing template, hopefully with extraordinary results.

When I read about the efficacy of the ultraviolet light wavelength 380 nanometres, I wondered if it was possible to use this unique wavelength multi-dimensionally and flood the subtle bodies with it. And if I could do this, would it impact on the physical body and if so, what would be the outcome?

Wow! I'm delighted to say it is an amazing healing template for working with the cells.

In the first instance, I only used it on myself then after getting some tangible results shared it with some clients to experiment with. This is what one of them wrote about the technique:

> "I have been visualising the internal treatment with the 380 nanometer UV light. I call it the 'A380' (like the aircraft) treatment. I don't know whether it is my imagination or not but there seems to be an overall improvement in the way I feel about the way I feel (if you know what I mean). Many of the previous symptoms/sensations have waned or disappeared since I have started thinking 'A380'. Maybe it is a combination of the A380 and the other things that I have been doing."

I have developed many healing templates with the 380 nanometer and this one is a particular favourite.

Template: 380 Nanometer Crystal Hut

On your screen of mind, imagine you are inside a crystal hut (it is the shape of a cylinder with a cone on top as the roof). The sun is shining brightly in the midday sky and the crystal filters the sunlight allowing only the light vibration of 380 nanometers to penetrate the crystal and you. Receive the rich healing of the 380 nanometers and stay there as long as you need to.

Experiment with this healing template. Observe if you experience a tangible shift in your health? To maintain any transformation repeat this template regularly.

Where does illness or disease begin

Master Cells in the Body

The power of each cell has fascinated me for over 20 years and I pondered the concept of master cells in the body.

I thought about this a lot and wondered if Master Cells ("MC's") existed could they be in charge of the division process within their own sub-group? And if you could heal each "MC", could you conceivably heal your body working with a small number of cells.

These questions intrigued me, particularly as I was creating illness within my own body which I wanted to heal. With curiosity, I meditated with these questions in mind and experienced the following technique which has been successfully duplicated by many people.

In a vision, I was shown there are 10 MC's within the human body and the following process could be used to heal them. I've recently wondered whether these Master Cells are part of the stem cell system. It's an interesting consideration.

When I received these instructions to heal the MC's, I was very unwell and only 2 out of 10 cells appeared perfectly round. Over the years, this number has varied on each inspection.

We live in a stressful time and it is not enough to do this treatment just the once. Stress impacts us energetically every day and it is wise to check your 10 MC's at least once a month – preferably once a week – to make sure they are all perfectly round.

Template: Master Cell Healing

- Be seated in a comfortable position (on a cushion, meditation stool or chair).
- Take a deep breath in through the base chakra drawing that breath all the way up through the chakras to the top of your shoulders. Hold it for the count of 5 and gently release the breath, letting go of all negativity and thoughts of the day – repeat 2 more times.

The Art of Self-Healing

- Breathing normally, imagine you are walking along a pathway and come to a set of stairs. There are seven steps before you and as you walk down each step a colour shoots up and surrounds you. Breathe in this colour all the way to the bottom of your lungs and gently release all the way out before stepping down onto the next step. The colours of the steps are as follows:

  RED
      ORANGE
          YELLOW
              GREEN
                  BLUE
                        PURPLE
                            VIOLET

- At the bottom of the steps is a beautiful golden doorway with an ornate handle. Put your hand on the handle and open the door to find an incredible bright golden light that shines out to meet you. Step into this light, breathing it all the way into your lungs and releasing any last residue of negativity and the outside world as you continue walking through the golden light.

- After taking 7 steps, you step into a room that you can decorate creatively and spontaneously as you want. However, there is one item that is required in this room. A very large screen.

- **Through creative and spontaneous visualisation you will heal your "10 MC's".** Remember creative visualisation is where you manipulate the image before your mind's eye. Spontaneous visualisation is where an image appears in your mind's eye without conscious thought (a bit of a surprise really!).

- Instruct your "1st MC" to appear on your screen (because you have given this instruction you are to wait for it to arrive spontaneously). Inspect the cell - if it is not perfectly round, make it round using creative visualisation. You can be as outrageous and adventurous as you want in this process to keep your cell perfectly round. There

Where does illness or disease begin

are no boundaries or limits in this dimension. *On my first visit I used building scaffolding to hold my changes in place. Another time, I popped a road pipe inside the cell to keep it round.*

- Instruct your "2nd MC" to appear on your screen. Repeat as for "1st MC". Repeat the process above until you have reviewed your "10 MC's" and are confident they are all perfectly round.

Now, for the most important part:

- Look at your "10 MC's" on your **viewing screen** and creatively see a small candle flame flickering in the centre of each cell. Focus intently on this flame and watch it grow larger and brighter the more you focus, until the entire cell is filled completely with the flame.

- When this occurs within all of them, the cells disappear from the screen in a flash of bright light leaving the screen blank. The healing is now being done.

- Find the doorway you came in through at the beginning of your treatment. Open the door and step back into the bright golden light, breathe it all the way into your lungs and all the way out - completing the healing process. Take 7 steps through the bright golden light onto the stairs with the coloured lights shining up from each step.

- Walk slowly up the stairs, with each step that you take the colour recedes back into the step, starting with violet through to red:

RED
ORANGE
YELLOW
GREEN
BLUE
PURPLE
VIOLET

- You are all the way back now on the pathway where you began. Take a deep breath in and gently release as you come all the way back into your body. Move your hands and feet and open your eyes when you are ready.

You are now back in the room where you began this healing treatment.

Do you feel lighter than when you started your treatment? Does your body feel energized?

Stress

There are different types of stress that impact the body/mind. Some are good, some not so good.

Have you heard the phrase "fight or flight"? This is referred to as **survival stress** and it is a good thing to have if your life is in danger. When your body senses danger it sends out a rush of adrenalin which gives you the surge of energy to stay and fight or get away from the situation (flight).

Another type of stress is **internal stress** and it is not good for your health and wellbeing. It is generally referred to as worry and is often linked with things we can't control or things we know are going to cause stress.

Environmental stress is your response to things going on around you, such as noise, crowds, traffic, and pressure from work or family. Identifying these stressors and learning how to avoid them will help you bring your stress levels down.

Then there is **fatigue and overwork.** This stress builds up over time and is more difficult to manage as often the root problem is poor time management.[3]

The combination of stress, worry and emotion = energy blockages in the cells of your body. The sooner these blockages are released, the quicker your body will return to its optimal health.

There are many ways to release stress from your body:

- Walk in nature.
- Take a siesta regularly.

Where does illness or disease begin

- Unplug from the communication grid – yes, that means turn your phone, computer, iPad and television OFF.
- Sit down at the dining table and eat your meal in a relaxed way.
- Have stimulating conversations – exclude politics and religion from the agenda.
- Listen to your favourite music – LOUDLY!
- Dance .
- Yoga, pilates, Tai Chi.
- Take a lunch break for 1 hour away from your work environment.
- Meditate regularly.
- Watch a funny movie.
- Read a novel.
- Have a massage.
- Go for a swim, preferably in the ocean or a lake.
- Swing in a hammock while reading a book or simply have a snooze.
- Gardening, either your own garden or at your local community garden.
- Play board games or cards.
- Get down on the floor and play with children.

The list is endless; all you have to do is give yourself permission to do them.

Next time you see someone doing one of these things don't criticise them for being lazy, or look at them with envy. Go on and do it yourself!

Another way of releasing stress and tension from your body is to work with a qualified practitioner.

The Art of Self-Healing

Exercise: Release Stress and Anxiety

Worry is a key contributor to stress. To release stress and anxiety, locate what you are worried about. Score your stress out of 10 eg., 8:10

- Stand in front of the mirror. Place you right hand on your thymus gland. It is located behind the sternum (chest plate) and between your lungs.
- Look into your eyes in your reflection and say out loud in reference to the worry: "*I don't have to do that anymore!*"
- Repeat these words.
- Repeat again, this time really mean it and convince your reflection.
- Do you feel warmth flooding through your chest and then move through your body?
- If yes, go to the last step. If no, repeat the above step until you do.
- Wait a couple of minutes and check in with self to see if your stress levels have dropped. What score do you give yourself now?
- If the score is higher than 5 place your hand on your thymus gland and ask yourself is there anything you could be doing you are not doing which is causing you stress.
- Look at your reflection and say out loud in reference to this "thing" you are not doing: "*I can do that!*"
- Repeat these words.
- Repeat again, this time really mean it and convince your reflection.
- Do you feel warmth flooding through your chest and then moving through your body?
- If yes, go to the last step. If no, repeat the above step until you do.
- Wait a couple of minutes and check in with self to see if your stress levels have dropped. What score do you give yourself now?

- If you are still above 5:10 look for a different source of stress and repeat either or both processes again.

This template works very effectively. I recommend this to be one of your priority templates for living a balanced, harmonious life if you are prone to stress and anxiety. It is a resource to be used regularly.

The Art of Self-Healing

Chapter 12
Unique Healing Templates

This is my favourite part of vibrational healing. Somewhere along the journey I discovered the body responds profoundly to visualisation and often the more abstract, absurd or magnified it is the more impact it has on the body.

The ways to heal the body through creative and spontaneous visualisation are endless. In Chapter 4 you learned about the different types of visualisation and now I'll show you how to use them with extraordinary results.

The healing templates being shared here all use visualization. You don't literally do these tasks – you visualize or imagine doing them to your holographic or energy body – unless you are specifically instructed to do something physically. These templates are ones that have been used repeatedly with success. Test them for yourself.

The Alimentary Canal

The whole alimentary canal can experience problems of one sort or another. There can be a problem with the oesophagus – mostly reflux which can go on to cause oesophagitis or inflammation of the oesophagus. Sometimes reflux is referred to as heart burn.

Moving further down the canal into the stomach, many people experience problems here. The most common problem is ulcers. There are different types of ulcers and different causes.

One particular ulcer condition is caused by the bacteria **Helicobacter pylori**. This is easily treatable with antibiotics. However, if left untreated in some cases it is considered part of the process in the stomach cancer cycle.

The alimentary canal moves from the stomach to the duodenum. This is the first part of the small intestine and is where most of the chemical digestion takes place. Ulcers can occur in this part of the intestines as well and they are called duodenal ulcers.

If you have persistent stomach problems and suspect you have an ulcer, I strongly recommend you have investigations done – such as a gastroscopy or sometimes known as an endoscopy. This is an invasive procedure and requires sedation, but it is the most sensitive test available for diagnosing ulcers or inflammation of the oesophagus and stomach.

There are other conditions of the small and large intestines such as Crohn's disease, colitis, ulcerative colitis, gastritis and coeliac disease. They all affect the lining of the bowel.

There is another test called a colonoscopy which allows the surgeon to see your bowel with a camera.

If you are concerned about the health of your alimentary canal – any part – you do need to speak to your doctor and tell them your symptoms. If an endoscopy or colonoscopy is recommended – do these tests.

I am a great believer in having these tests done. If I hadn't done these tests, I may have progressed to bowel cancer by now. Be sensitive to your body and be practical with the actions you take. For me personally I was experiencing abdominal pain and I had a colonoscopy.

Thankfully I didn't ignore these symptoms – during several colonoscopies tubular adenomas were removed from my bowel. I am delighted to share with you – I am now down to 5 yearly follow ups (instead of yearly) as my last colonoscopy and the one before was clear. I no longer experience any persistent abdominal pain.

It's pretty exciting to see how I have been able to transform my bowel. Hopefully you can transform your bowel if this is a problem area for you.

Please do get a medical diagnosis of any concerns you have.

Once a diagnosis is given – and hopefully you don't have any nasty problems such as cancer, I recommend you use this process to heal the lining of the canal – from mouth to anus.

This is the technique I developed for someone who had ulcerative colitis or Crohn's disease. I can't remember which condition it was. This template made a tremendous difference for him. He was facing having a big section of his bowel removed. My understanding is after doing this process he was told he didn't need that surgery. This was a really good outcome.

If you have a condition like this – you still have to manage it with practical methods, too. You must manage your stress levels, be discerning with what you eat and do this visualisation work.

Your body responds to images and the feeling intention you connect with these images. The more healing visualisation you do, the more your body responds to it.

[**WARNING: If you are concerned about your oesophagus, stomach, intestines or bowel seek the advice of your medical practitioner.**]

Template: Alimentary Canal Healing

This process lines the inside of the alimentary canal with a sheath.

Imagine you have the beginning of the sheath in your mouth. It looks like a clear plastic skin and it begins to unravel in your mouth and lines the entire canal from the mouth, down the oesophagus, balloons out to line the stomach, down into the duodenum and continues through the small intestine, into the large intestine and through to the anus.

Once you have done this, imagine you have a huge bucket of white cream. You need to cover the entire sheath you have placed in your alimentary canal with this cream. It is similar to icing a cake with a layer of icing.

The next step is to bring another layer through the canal. It is almost like sausage skin. Take that from mouth to anus and you can do this quite quickly as the dimension you are working in to do these visualisations doesn't have the constraints of our physical reality. You can warp speed your visualisations.

What you have ended up with now is skin, cream, skin. Continue this process until you have 10-20 layers. I'm not going to give you a definite number here – you need to feel into this intuitively and determine what would be best for you and your current situation.

Once you have visualised as many layers as you intuitively feel is needed – flood the entire alimentary canal with emerald green light. Track the light from the mouth, down the oesophagus, into the stomach, through the small and large intestine and out the back passage.

When this is complete – repeat the process with bright white light – and when you reach the anus there will be what feels or looks like an explosion of bright light. Take a deep breath in. As you gently release the breath come all the way through the light back into your body and into the room.

This light phase of the process sets the healing. You'll find I use the emerald green light followed by bright white light with every healing template.

This technique is not a once off template. If you have an alimentary problem, I recommend you repeat this process daily until you scan your entire alimentary canal and you see and feel it as being a healthy system.

Each time you repeat a template you show your body how to heal itself. You are building new neural pathways and empowering your body with more energy, vitality and dimensional resources.

Irritable Bowel Syndrome

Irritable bowel syndrome is an unpleasant condition to experience. Why does it happen? I don't know for sure. It is somewhat of a mystery. However, I suspect it is about trapped emotion linked with food intolerances, allergies and sensitivities.

I am not going to go into the ins and outs of IBS. If you have this you are well aware of the consequences of it and may even have a protocol that works for you.

Having personally experienced IBS for the better part of 30 years – which seems to run in our family, in desperation I had to develop a protocol that worked for me, particularly to help with the bowel spasms.

One of the IBS symptoms that happens is what I call the stomach dump. The top part of the small intestines dumps the food too quickly into the rest of the intestines and the bowel urgently needs to evacuate. These episodes of diarrhea can be energetically draining if they persist.

If you suffer from persistent diarrhea and you have been diagnosed with IBS speak to your doctor or pharmacist about what can assist you. If you have not been diagnosed with IBS and suffer persistent diarrhea you also need to speak with your doctor about this.

The most intolerable symptom of IBS for me is the bowel spasms.

These are my observations about why and when the bowel spasms.

One of the most significant causes of bowel spasms is gluten and this is found in wheat, spelt, kumut, rye, barley, oats (although it is believed oats is simply contaminated by other gluten grains – and if the oats is kept free from contaminants can be eaten). If you suspect you are intolerant or allergic to gluten – stop eating it. Do you feel better? It seems anyone who is diagnosed with IBS or CFS (chronic fatigue syndrome) one of the first things to be tested is allergy/intolerance to gluten.

This is a decision you need to make. It is a simple blood test these days.

Getting back to the bowel spasms. Another factor which you may not have been aware of is when your body temperature drops below a certain level the bowel can spasm causing gas to be trapped in pockets which can be extremely painful. For me personally, these episodes are right up there with the pain of childbirth.

Here is my solution to manage these episodes?

Template: IBS Spasm Healing

Firstly, if your core body temperature goes lower than normal – and this can happen if the early morning cools down and you don't have enough bed covers. You need to warm up your core body temperature quickly. One of the best ways to do this is to wrap a thin blanket around your abdomen or use a (covered) hot water bottle on your abdomen.

It may also be that you have inadvertently eaten gluten and you are having a reaction to the gluten as it hits your lower bowel. Gluten can take hours to many hours to reach this part of your bowel.

If you don't monitor your gluten intake, I recommend you trial eliminating gluten from your diet for at least one month to see what impact it has on your overall wellbeing – and particularly on your IBS.

Another problem for IBS sufferers is they can have too much roughage eg., from nuts. Dukkah – an Egyptian nut and spice mix can also trigger bowel spasms. Really it is a matter of observing how your body responds to foods.

Whatever the cause, you need a swift natural process for relieving the spasms.

The colour blue can be used to soothe the body. It has an anaesthetic quality which is very calming. The particular vibration of blue to use in this healing template is the blue of the midday sky in summer. It is a rich vital and vivid azure blue.

To do this process, be associated in your body. Imagine you have an azure blue ball of light about the size of a golf ball and place it inside your mouth. Swallow it.

From inside, track the ball of blue light as it goes down your oesophagus into your stomach, circulate it around the entire circumference of your stomach, into the duodenum, down into the small intestines and then into the large intestines (bowel) and out the back passage.

Sound simple?

When you are not doubled over in pain and you can barely breathe – yes, it's very simple. However, when you are in pain, it can be a challenge to complete the process in one go.

The secret to this technique being effective is you **must** stay 100% focused on the journey of the blue ball of light all the way from the mouth to the anus. If you get distracted by the pain, an outside thought or another vision other than the one I've described to you – **YOU MUST** return to the beginning of the template and start again.

You will need to practice this template regularly as it is the discipline your body will respond to as well as the colour. Your bowel will naturally relax when you initiate this healing template.

In most cases, with practice you will be able to stop the spasms within 1-2 minutes or in a severe case within 5 minutes of using this template – particularly if you use the blanket or warm scarf around the abdomen as well. An added bonus is to release the gas from your bowel too.

However, this is not always possible unless you can train your bowel to relax using the above template or something else that has a similar effect.

Gallstones

In my time as a practicing medical intuitive, the most undiagnosed or misdiagnosed range of symptoms would have to be gallstones. I'm not sure why.

Gallstones can cause a multitude of symptoms that appear to be completely unrelated and can lead sufferers down many rabbit holes looking for a solution to their suffering.

I stick my hand up and admit this happened to me, too. One doctor told me I was depressed and wanted me to take anti-depressants. Seriously!

The symptoms of gallstones are:

- pain across the middle of the back
- painful right shoulder – sometimes misdiagnosed as frozen shoulder
- painful right arm

The Art of Self-Healing

- cramps in the legs
- nausea and vomiting
- headaches
- fatigue
- pain under the right ribs
- sore stomach / abdomen
- fever, chills and sweating
- foggy / woolly feeling in the head.

When you find out you have gallstones you may never have another attack – or you could continue to suffer.

When I was diagnosed with gallstones I was completely shocked and in denial. I was not inclined to see a surgeon or visit the hospital as my doctor requested. This was my first mistake.

I should have done this as soon as possible after being diagnosed, so I had a better understanding about the medical situation and how dangerous it can be. I haven't written this to frighten you, but to alert you to educate yourself about gallstones and any possible complications.

If a doctor says to you, *"Oh, not to worry your gallstones are small"*, you need to ask more questions. My understanding is the smaller ones can cause more problems than the large ones.

If you have large gallstones, it is possible to have surgery in China where the gallstones are removed from the gallbladder through keyhole surgery. You do not lose your gallbladder. If this is of interest to you research it on the internet.

There is an easy natural remedy you can try before committing to surgery. If you have concerns about using this remedy or other natural remedies, discuss it with your doctor or naturopath before going ahead.

I didn't know about this remedy when my gallstones were diagnosed, plus I had a diseased gallbladder as well as gallstones, and had to have surgery.

Unique healing templates

Template: Gallstones Remedy

Make a mixture of 1/2 cold pressed extra virgin olive oil + 1/2 fresh lemon juice.

- This mixture tastes like a delicious salad dressing.
- Make small amounts – the most I would mix at any one time would be 1/8 cup of oil + 1/8 cup of lemon juice.

Take 1 dessertspoon 4 times a day – a dessertspoon at breakfast / lunch / dinner and before bed and **be sure to take it <u>with food</u>**.

Take this mixture for 14-21 days. And from between days 14-21 you should pass the gallstones through your bowels.

(Keep the mixture in the refrigerator – the older it becomes the thicker/creamier it will be – this is still fine to drink. It just doesn't look so palatable.)

[**NOTE: Seek medical advice immediately if you are concerned.**]

Anecdote

One of my elderly clients was bedridden and being treated for a blood disorder without success. She was most upset she was missing out on her bowls outings. After going to visit her and listening to her symptoms I was convinced she had gallstones. Not wanting to leave any stone unturned in helping her mother, the daughter searched the internet and found the above remedy. My elderly client took the remedy for 21 days – passed many gallstones and was back playing bowls in no time with all symptoms gone.

I cannot say that this remedy will work for everyone, but anecdotally it works.

Where your health is concerned – you must do all your research and talk to your health practitioner and make a decision that you are happy with.

Releasing Pain from the body

I will teach this template from the point of view of the shoulder. Go to

Chapter 5 to see what the different parts of the body represent so you can locate the particular thought process which has created the pain.

Many people have a problem with their shoulders. And yes, you could say there are a multitude of valid reasons for the problem.

From a metaphysical point of view, the shoulders represent taking on responsibility for other people's "stuff" or not taking responsibility for your own "stuff".

So, if you have or get sore shoulders, my question to you is what have you taken responsibility for since the shoulder started hurting? Generally, you will find the answer very quickly.

It is easy to let that go!

Let's say your shoulder suddenly becomes very painful around the time you make a decision about taking responsibility for someone else's "stuff". Perhaps you made the decision to move in with someone you know doesn't have much money and you suspect you will most likely be the one paying the bills. Either subconsciously or consciously you are taking on responsibility for the financial wellbeing of this person. If this is a conscious decision and you are happy to be doing this the chances of your shoulders becoming painful around this decision are slim.

However, if you subconsciously take on this responsibility and you're not aware you've done this or you have ignored the niggling doubts that have surfaced in your consciousness, suddenly you seem to have stepped into the pain factory.

This pain says you are not being congruent with your life path or purpose. In fact, if you did make this decision unconsciously I would be surprised if your shoulder doesn't become painful.

Here's the question, would you believe you can get rid of this debilitating pain in 1-2 minutes?

Unique healing templates

Template: Shoulder Pain Release

For your shoulder to be relieved of pain quickly place your opposite hand on your shoulder where it is sore. If this is not possible get as close as you can to it.

Search back through your memories and locate the decision you made around responsibility. Now say out loud:

"I don't have to do that anymore!"

And again.

"I don't have to do that anymore!"

And again and really convince someone that you mean it.

"I don't have to do that anymore!"

If you don't get a tingling feeling or a body sign letting you know those words are true, this technique hasn't worked. So dig deeper and keep saying the words till you get the feeling that you really believe what you're saying. Sometimes, it can take 6, 8 – 10 times. The amount of repetitions is not important. Repeat the words until you get the validation.

When I do this for myself, I get a warm tingling sensation run down my frontal line from my throat chakra to my base chakra. When this happens, I know the words are coming from a place of deep belief.

Here's the thing with this template, you must honour the commitment you have just made to yourself. If you don't honour your promise, guess what happens? The pain comes back.

It's not that the template doesn't work, you have forgotten your agreement which says you have a pattern of doing this and it may take some relapses to magnify the pattern enough for you to stop it altogether.

And that's not a bad thing. It simply means you need to repeat the process. Really **mean it** and **honour** it.

There is another possibility this template won't work and that is you haven't identified the root decision you made to create the pain. Go back through your memory and find another decision you've made around responsibility that doesn't sit well with you.

Repeat the process.

Did you think you were finished?

No, there is another side to the coin. For every yin there is a yang. The other scenario is you stepping up and taking action.

Ask yourself – *"What is it that I want to do and I'm not yet doing?"*

Locate that "thing" and place your hand on the part of your body that's in pain and say out loud:

"I can do that!"

And again!

"I can do that!"

And again – and really mean it. You either have to convince yourself or another person in the room.

"I can do that!"

It is the same scenario as above. If after 3 times the pain is still there keep going till you get the validation via a body sign that you believe what you are saying. The pain will leave your body.

The key to working with these decisions is they can be quite simple so don't feel that you have to psycho-analyse your life to locate them.

Personal story:

I made a decision not to mentor someone, but a third party asked me to reconsider. In my mind I thought maybe I'm being unreasonable and decided to do it. Within 24 hours my knee had swollen to twice the size, I couldn't walk very well and was in immense pain. It was so bad I booked into see my Bowen therapist the next day. Holy moly, I couldn't work out what I had done!

Sometimes I forget what I have at my fingertips. After 24 hours of intense pain, I remembered this particular template. I simply reversed the decision to mentor this person using the process above. Went to sleep and woke up in the morning with no swelling, no pain and very clear about my intentions.

Fluid Retention

This template is for the lymphatic system and reducing fluid retention in the body. I use what I call my **"Dr Shivago syringe"** and it looks a little like this.

Template: Fluid retention

Imagine you have a huge syringe and place it in the area where the lymphatic system is blocked or where there is swelling. Usually this is in the feet, ankles or underarm. However, you can get fluid retention in your face, and this can make you feel very unwell, too.

When you remove the fluid from your face, it is remarkable how the reduction of the pressure in your head makes you feel so much better.

Visualise inserting the syringe into the affected area and imagine you are drawing the syringe back and see the fluid flowing into the cylinder compartment. Keep drawing back until the syringe reaches its capacity. Remove the syringe and place it into a black box beside you.

Imagine inserting another syringe and repeat the process. Keep repeating the process until you are unable to draw fluid into the cylinder. Close the lid on the black box. The universe knows what to do with this waste.

It is extraordinary how effective this template is.

Many years ago I was asked if I would come to see a friend of a friend. This person was overcoming major surgery.

When I saw this person, I was concerned for their wellbeing. I couldn't see the outline of any bones in their feet. They looked like big fat sausages on the ends of legs. I was stunned to see how swollen they were.

I wondered, *"My goodness, what can I do to help this person!"*

I asked them to do the above template and they removed all the fluid into the syringes. This took a few minutes and then we started talking about something else.

I also taught them some other resources to help themself.

Within 15 minutes their feet and hands looked normal, I could see all of the bones. It was a remarkable phenomenon to witness.

When something like this happens it feels like a miracle, but basically what you have done is shown the body how to remove the fluid.

Recently I worked with someone who had blocked lymphatic glands under their arms and down the sides of the ribs. They would get sore spots. I asked them to do this very same process and within 30-60 seconds, they said, *"Oh, the pain is all gone!"*

This is something you can do to manage the fluid retention in your body or to aid your lymphatic system. I personally use it whenever I need to. I love it when my toes are wrinkly because I know there is no fluid retention there. It feels awesome.

This is a testimonial from one of my friends, Terrie, who I helped out:

Complicated Pain Syndrome Healed

"In November 2011, I broke my left wrist and ended up with complications. CPS - Complicated Pain Syndrome; pain medications and rehab. I was advised by medical experts that this condition has about a two year recovery period.

On January 5th 2012, the lovely Julie came to visit. At this stage, Julie was unaware of my medical condition. Before leaving Julie asked if she could do a healing. I was extremely hesitant because of the pain. The thought of anyone touching my wrist was unthinkable. Trusting in Julie, we sat on the lounge and she instructed me on how to breathe and channel my thought processes into a specific direction.

Without coming into direct contact with my wrist, Julie started working with me. After twenty minutes to half an hour, my goodness, the swelling had reduced dramatically through my hand and fingers. Movement was happening. I could move my wrist. Incredible! I have now returned to work. Pain is fleeting and almost non-existent. A big thank you to Julie."

Terrie has also been able to return to motor bike riding and is very happy with the results of this healing session.

I can't speak highly enough about the benefits of this healing template. You can do it for yourself.

Infection Template

This infection template was developed when someone saw me on TV and rang to say her friend was in hospital and had been there for 8 weeks. They had been involved in an accident that had crushed their ankle. Doctors inserted a pin into the ankle to keep it stable.

Unfortunately, their body was rejecting the pin and they had a persistent infection in the area with an ongoing fever. On this particular Thursday, the doctor advised if the fever and infection were not gone by the following Monday they would have to amputate.

The result of this template was that not only did the infection resolve within the 3 days, but my client was discharged from hospital. The fever was gone within 12 hours and in 3 days they had healed completely.

This template has kept people out of hospital, let them go home early and escalated healing in many others. It is useful for all types of infection or blood disorders. The process cleans the blood of any particles that do not serve a healthy body.

I recommend you keep this healing template on your list of top healing resources, as you can use it for many and varied reasons. If in doubt, do this one. Some examples of when to use it:

- anytime there is pus
- when you've been diagnosed with an infection eg., pneumonia, tonsillitis
- when you have a high fever
- low grade infections
- cold, flu, virus.

However, do be sensible with your health. Sometimes you need to use modern or natural medicine in conjunction with this form of vibrational healing.

At 4pm on 9th August 2013, I was diagnosed with pneumonia and bronchitis. The doctor gave me 2 types of penicillin to treat the infection as he wasn't sure which bacteria was the culprit.

I had a 3 day x 1:1 residential retreat scheduled to start on the Sunday afternoon. My client, who was a doctor, was comfortable with coming on retreat with me coughing from pneumonia and bronchitis. So the retreat went ahead.

Over the next week, I diligently used the following template as often as I thought of it as well as took all my penicillin. On the following Saturday morning, just 8 days after being diagnosed with pneumonia and bronchitis I woke up completely healed. It was the fastest recovery I have ever had from a chest infection.

It would be over 2 years before I caught another cold or flu. There was another template I used at this time which worked on my DNA. This DNA template has had a profound impact on my health and wellness and I share it later in the chapter.

Template: Infection Healing

With this template you program your immune system to keep anything that is not for your highest good out of your blood stream. Use this template anytime you are concerned about having an infection or being vulnerable to infection – particularly if you need to stay in hospital for any reason.

Imagine or feel the essence of you travel from your lungs into the blood vessel that takes the oxygen filled blood from your lungs to your heart.

It should feel or look like you are in a tunnel that has a red liquid flowing through it. As you become sensitive to the change in light you may notice that you can actually see or feel the different cells in the blood.

Imagine or feel a gold panning sieve being placed in this tunnel. This is a magic sieve and will only allow through the mesh, cells and nutrients which help you stay healthy and safe. The mesh catches anything that could harm you.

Say this prayer to activate the magic sieve:

"Beloved guardians of the sieve please activate the miracle of this sieve and only allow the cells and nutrients that will help keep me healthy and safe to pass through your wire mesh. I ask that this activation stay in place as long as my body needs it. Amen".

If you are using this template to prevent against infection you can stop here.

However, if you have an infection you will see or feel the sieve filling with all the things that are not serving your wellbeing. There isn't a particular way this will look. It will be unique in each circumstance.

When the sieve is almost full, place another sieve behind it, remove the full sieve from your tunnel and place it into a black box. From here, it will be safely disposed of by the Universe.

The activation prayer takes care of everything for you.

When the sieve is no longer being filled with infection, feel yourself being gently drawn into the bright Divine Light, come all the way back into the room

The Art of Self-Healing

and into your body.

I couldn't tell you how many people have learned and used this process. One of my greatest joys has been to be told how it has kept children with infection out of hospital. They manage to treat whatever is causing the fever with this template. I'm not suggesting you don't go to the doctor or not use allopathic methods of treating yourself or your family, but use this template first or in combination with other treatments.

It is quite an extraordinary process and is a hugely powerful healing template.

I use it for any infection in the body or even for cancer. Particularly if it is blood cancer to sift the cancer cells out of the blood.

I believe you can clean your blood of infection, bacteria and viruses using this process.

Don't just limit this template to humans. You can use it successfully on animals, too.

I would love to gift a recording of this template to you. Go to Insight Timer insig.ht/gm_1273.

DNA Codon Activation

This is the second healing template I used to heal from pneumonia in 2013. I stumbled upon a transcript of an interview with Drunvalo Melchizedek by Diane Cooper called Children of the New Dream. The full interview seems to pop up on many websites if you Google it.

The interview was transformative for me. Drunvalo spoke about a new group of children being born around the world and here is a copy of the paragraphs that had the most impact:

"It is ... the "Children of AIDS." About 10 or 11 years ago in the US, there was a baby born with AIDS. They tested him at birth and at 6 months and he tested positive for AIDS. They tested him a year later and he still tested positive. Then they didn't test him again until he was 6, and what was amazing is that this test showed that he

Unique healing templates

was completely AIDS free! In fact, there was no trace that he ever had AIDS or HIV whatsoever! He was taken to UCLA to see what was going on and those tests showed that he didn't have normal human DNA.

In the human DNA we have 4 nucleic acids that combine in sets of 3 producing 64 different patterns that are called codons. Human DNA all over the world always has 20 of these codons turned on and the rest of them are turned off, except for 3 which are the stop and start codes, much like a computer. Science always assumed that the ones that were turned off were old programs from our past. I've always seen them like application programs in a computer. Anyway...this boy had 24 codons turned on — 4 more than any other human being. Then they tested this kid to see how strong his immune system was. They took a very lethal dose of AIDS in a petri dish and mixed it with some of his cells and his cells remained completely unaffected. They kept raising the lethalness of the composition and finally went up to 3,000 times more than what was necessary to infect a human being and his cells stayed completely disease free.

... I have gone into the merkabah and asked my subconscious mind to change my codons in the same way and ever since I began to do this over two years ago, I haven't been able to get sick. I don't know if I've been able to change them or not. I guess the only way I'd know is with a DNA test. However, I've been exposed to all kinds of things and when someone gets sick I purposely get close to them and try to get it. I've been trying to get sick — and I can feel something come on — it will last maybe an hour and then it's gone."

This was enough information for me to decide I wanted to turn on my extra 4 codons. As with all my templates they happen spontaneously in the first instance. Here is the DNA Codon Activation Template. The small group of people I have taught this to have experienced a potent impact.

Template: DNA Codon Activation

- Step into your sacred creation temple. On your screen of mind imagine a double helix DNA strand. Inside the strand is a lift. Step inside the lift and press level 21. You will start this template with the presumption your 20 codons of normal DNA are switched on.

- Watch the buttons on the lift as you shoot up to level 21. As you go past each level the lift button should light up. Take note if any button does not light up. You will go back and fix this later.

- When you get to level 21, the doors open and you see a concrete ledge with a pipe at eye height. This pipe represents your codon. If there is a button/plug pushed into the pipe, this codon is switched off. Take the button/plug out of the pipe and put it on the ledge at your feet – this turns the codon on and allows the energy to flow.

- Take a deep breath in and feel what happens in your physical body. You may feel energy activate somewhere. This is a spontaneous experience and not one to fake or copy.

- Step back into the lift and press level 22. Repeat the process as above.

- Repeat for Level 23 and Level 24.

- Step back into the lift. If you had any buttons between G-20 which didn't light up on the journey up to Level 21, go back and check to see if the button/plug is pushed in or out. Pull it out and put it on the ledge if you need to.

- Once all levels have the button/plug pulled out – go back to Level 24 and press G. As the lift goes down to Ground emerald green light shines out of each lift button as you pass that floor.

- When you get to Ground, the doors open and bright white light rushes into the lift. Step into the light and hear the doors close behind you. The lift shoots back up to Level 24 taking the bright white light to each level setting the DNA activation.

- You keep walking through the light, back into your physical body and into the room where you started. Come all the way back into your body and if you need to ground yourself, place the palm of your hand over your crown chakra at the top of your head for a few minutes.

You may need to repeat this template 5 times (1 per day for 5 days) for the DNA Activation to become stable. After you've completed the 5 Activations,

Unique healing templates

check in once per month to confirm the 24 codons remain switched on.

In Drunvalo's interview he said that he tries to get sick. He can feel it come on, but within an hour he is fine again. This has also been my experience for the past 2 years since I had pneumonia and I did this DNA Codon Activation. Give it a go, I would love to know what happens.

Full Body Tune Up

I love this particular template. It is similar to taking a tonic or having a complete tune up. Again, the process involves using creative and spontaneous visualisation.

This template is one that came to me after a client contacted me to say her mother was in intensive care and the doctors didn't know what was wrong with her and didn't know how to fix her.

She asked me if I would intervene. After her mother gave permission for me to work on her from a distance this template is what unfolded during her session.

Template: Full Body Tune up

Have you ever watched a magic show where the magician floats his assistant in a horizontal position seemingly floating in the air? To prove there are "no strings", the magician passes a hoop over the suspended body.

This template requires you to see yourself on your screen of mind suspended in mid-air. Imagine a hoop being passed very slowly over your body from head to toe. As you do this, coloured lights spontaneously emit from inside the hoop sending light vibration through your body.

It may be a single colour or a rainbow of colours. This is the spontaneous element of the template. Don't instruct the hoop what colour light to use. Simply witness the colours your body needs to heal.

Your task is to imagine the hoop slowly passing over the body. If there is an area of the body which needs a lot of healing work, the hoop will move very slowly – and there will be a lot of colour activity. Sometimes it doesn't seem to be moving at all – just wait – when the healing is complete the hoop will start moving again.

This is not a process you can rush. The timing will be as it needs to go. It may take 10 minutes to half an hour in human time; or it may only take 2 minutes. There is no timeline. Simply as little or as much time as needed.

Sometimes you'll notice there are parts of the body the hoop skims over quite quickly. This means you don't need healing in this part of the body.

Allow the hoop to travel from head to toe as slow or fast as it needs to go and in whatever colour spontaneously shows up.

When the hoop has completely traversed the body, go back to the beginning and instruct the hoop to pass over the body again. If all the healing has been done, the hoop glides smoothly over the body. If there is more healing to be done, the hoop takes its time again.

The whole purpose of this template is to get your body to the point where the hoop glides over it from head to toe very smoothly. And this is your signal that the tune up has been completed.

The really interesting outcome of using this template on the elderly woman was the very next morning after this treatment; she was released from hospital (and from intensive care) because she had miraculously healed overnight.

Hmmm, was this a result of the work I did? We won't ever know. The daughter believes so.

About 9 months later, the daughter rang me again and said, *"Mum's back in intensive care and they don't know what's wrong with her!"*

I told her, *"Your Mum is worrying!"*

She was worrying and it was causing her health problem. Again, I was given permission to use this healing template. Amazingly the next day she was able to go home from hospital.

Will this work for you? I don't know. However, it is something I do on

Unique healing templates

myself regularly and it is an extraordinary process. I encourage you to do this several times a year or more regularly if you are not feeling very well and see what impact it has on you.

Template: Burn healing

This template came about after I heard a story about a man who said he healed a burn he received from a burst radiator on his car. He didn't share how he healed the burn. However, it was enough for me to hear the story (and this is a little tip for you – if you hear about someone somewhere in the world who has achieved a result, presume you have the capacity to achieve it as well with your natural self-healing ability).

One afternoon in 1990, I decided to cook donuts for the children. I had a large pot of very hot oil boiling away on the stove. I had just made my first donut. I proudly plucked it out of the oil and held it up to the light to admire my handiwork.

Yikes!!!!! The boiling oil ran off the donut, down the inside of the tongs between my fingers and over the back of my hand. As you can imagine it was excruciatingly painful. I ran cold water over my hand. The pain was intense.

Beside myself with pain I remembered the story I had been told. I sat quietly on the sofa and placed my good hand over the burn. I took a deep breath in and as I gently released the breath I imagined I could see the burn from the inside.

I flooded it with blue light because I knew blue light acted as an anaesthetic. I wondered, *"How am I going to heal this burn?"*

An image popped into my head of a transverse section of the burn on my hand. I could see where the burn affected the skin and gradually receded to healthy skin.

Spontaneously a roll of plastic cling wrap appeared in my vision and I intuitively knew this was a layer of new skin. I pulled a sheet of plastic wrap skin from the roll and lay it under the burn on the good skin.

Intuitively, I added a layer of white cream – completely covering the new skin. And then added another layer of skin over the white cream. In a manner similar to making lasagne.

The burn actually looked like a crater in the transverse image. I continued with the flat layers until the crater was filled – it took approximately 40 layers. Intuitively, I flooded the layers from the top to the bottom with emerald green light.

I use emerald green light because it sets the intention for healing. After this, I flooded the vision with bright white light to complete the healing. As it reached the bottom of the crater there was an enormous alchemical flash and the healing was complete. Using the flash as a catalyst, the essence of me travelled back into my body.

Interestingly, when I finished this process, the redness which had spread out around the burn had disappeared and the intense pain was gone. However, there was still a red mark where it was severely burnt which incidentally didn't blister.

Within half an hour, I was moving my hand around and had forgotten about the burn.

Another interesting phenomenon, the next morning the burn area had changed to a deep burgundy colour. Within a couple of days this disappeared and I forgot about the burn.

Two weeks later, the skin peeled like sunburn where the major burn had been. There was no scar or evidence of a burn.

This outcome was very exciting for me. And I wondered if I could duplicate the healing process. And yes, I could.

Phillip's Burn

My cousin came to stay with us while he attended his TAFE study to be a butcher. He came home one Friday with an ugly looking wound on the side of his ankle.

Quite concerned, I asked, *"What have you done?"*

"I burnt it at work!"

Did you know at the end of each day the butchers hose out the butchery with boiling water? They also hose off their rubber wellington boots. Unfortunately for Phillip, the boiling water went inside his wellington and burned his ankle.

He put aloe vera cream on the burn immediately.

He had a shower to wash the cream off so I could have a closer look. When he came out from the shower, it looked like he had a cricket ball filled with water attached to his ankle.

I took him straight to the doctor who drained the fluid out with a syringe and told him there was a third degree burn under the blister.

Phillip was prescribed 4 hourly Paracetamol (pain medication), given a week off work, told to keep his feet up and to go back and see the doctor every day for the following week to have the burn dressed.

I took him home and courageously said, *"I can fix that burn for you. I have a technique I'm working on."*

Phillip agreed to let me practice on him. It took me about 10 minutes to complete the healing template. He said he could feel something happening during the process.

I followed the same process as above and after I had finished Phillip said all the pain was gone. Yes!!! The healing removed all the pain, he didn't use any Paracetamol and just like on my hand, overnight the bad part of the burn turned burgundy and no further blistering occurred. When I took him back to the doctor the next morning, the doctor said, *"Hmmm, I've made a mistake. You don't have a third degree burn, but keep your feet up and take Paracetamol 4 hourly."*

Instead of resting we went sightseeing and then to a wedding with Phillip wearing new shoes.

Phillip could touch his burn 48 hours after it happened. There were no complications and was healing exceptionally well.

It had healed so well, he went back to work on the Monday. Unfortunately, he had to wear his wellington boots and the hard rubber of the boots broke the new skin. The healing became fractured and got infected. So, he still had to take the week off work.

The wound got very messy because of this setback. So, I did more healing on it and the result was good. If he hadn't worn the wellington boots the healing process would have been amazing.

Jamie's Burn

Mum called to say my nephew had pulled a cup of hot black coffee off the bench over his chest and arm. It had just been made so was very hot.

One of my daughter's school friends had done exactly the same thing at a similar age – about 2 – and she had scarring all over her chest and down her arm where she'd been burnt.

My sister took Jamie to the hospital and he was given a regime of what she had to do with him. She was to bring him back twice a day for so many days and then once a day for a certain time and then every couple of days. It was a 6 week healing protocol.

Mum asked if I could do something. I did this burn healing template on him (from a distance – there was about 2,000km between us) and he only needed to go to the hospital for several days to have dressings changed. He doesn't have any scars.

Hot Oil Burn

A friend of mine rang to say she answered the phone leaving oil on the stove on the highest setting. She completely forgot about it as she got caught up on the call.

The oil burst into flames setting off the fire alarm. Her husband raced upstairs, grabbed the saucepan of flaming oil, and ran through the house to throw it over the balcony. The boiling oil splashed onto his hand and wrist.

The burns were very bad and my friend asked if I could do something. I used the same template from a distance. The burns healed within days without scarring.

This is a very powerful healing template. I have taught this to many people who have had similar results.

Fireplace Burns

We have a wood fireplace and often I burn myself as I put the wood in the fire. When I use the template I don't scar and the burns heal very well. If I don't use the template, I get scars and sometimes infection.

There is something magical about this template and I recommend you use it for all burns.

Other Skin Conditions

The burn healing template can be used on other skin conditions as well. If you suffer from eczema, psoriasis, acne – anything to do with the skin, you can also heal these conditions from the inside out.

Template: Clunky or crunchy shoulder

This is another template which works very well.

Sometimes you may feel like you have a clunky shoulder or you can't lift your shoulder up as high as you want to. It feels like you have a restriction inside your shoulder joint. Or it may even crunch when you move it.

This is a creative visualisation process where you travel inside the shoulder socket via your screen of mind. The ball and the socket look something like a cup. As you travel inside your shoulder you keep an eye out for gravel or sand or there may be lumps on the socket or the ball.

If you find sand or gravel, imagine you can vacuum up any loose material with the universal vacuum cleaner which spontaneously appears in your visualisation. After you've done this, imagine you have some fine sandpaper and sand all the rough areas until they are smooth.

When everything feels smooth, that is no lumps or restriction of any sort, imagine you have an Aladdin's lamp filled with golden oil. It has a magnificent texture and actually oozes a little bit when you pour it out onto a very soft cloth.

Use this oily cloth to polish everything in your vision ie., the shoulder ball, the socket and surrounding area.

Once you have polished everything, infuse the whole vision with emerald green light to set the healing and finish with a bright white light. Wait for the alchemical flash and come back into your body. Take a deep breath and gently release. Open your eyes when you are ready.

Move your shoulder around. How does it feel? Hopefully it feels amazing and moves freely. If not, repeat the process.

Anxiety

Many people suffer from anxiety. I'm not going to go into the treatment of this from a professional point of view. Please seek professional advice if you are not coping.

This is a simple visualisation that impacts profoundly and holistically.

I call this template flower balancing.

When you use this process, you centre your horizontal and vertical energy. When these energies are out of balance you may experience anxiety, nausea, difficulty breathing and feeling out of control.

The flower balancing template helps you feel calm, reduces or eliminate nausea, breathe more easily and feel balanced.

If you are in a crisis situation you may need to repeat this exercise frequently – even as often as every few minutes.

Template: Flower Balancing for anxiety

Make yourself comfortable and imagine or if you can't visualise, feel that you are a seagull flying out over the ocean. There is no land in sight. All you

Unique healing templates

can see or feel is the sky and the water.

Become conscious of the ocean. *What does the water look or feel like? Is it rough? Is it smooth? Is it choppy? Are there white caps?* Make a mental note of how the ocean looks or feels when you spontaneously arrive above it.

Visualise or simply feel the ocean as smooth as glass. All you can see is the smooth blue ocean and the radiant blue sky as you hover above the water. You may even see the sunlight sparkling on the glass like surface.

Leave that scene.

Imagine or if you can't do this feel a beautiful bed of gerberas. Gerberas are flowers with a long thin stem and a colored head with fine petals – similar to a sunflower head. Take a note or feel how the gerberas are growing. *Are the stems straight and tall or are some or all of them leaning over or broken?* Whatever they look or feel like – use your creative mind to make all the gerberas stand up straight and tall facing the midday sun. Use whatever means you creatively intuit to do this.

Flick back to the ocean where you were before and make sure the water is still as smooth as glass. If it isn't make it smooth again.

Change the scene again and imagine you are standing at the edge of a canyon precipice with a rope bridge across it.

Yes, you are going to imagine yourself walking across that rope bridge. The design of the bridge is completely up to you. Feel the fear and walk across despite the fear. When you reach the other side, turn back and look at what you have achieved. Amazingly, the rope bridge transforms into a solid golden bridge.

Walk across the bridge and into the brightest light you could ever imagine. This is the Divine Source. You have now balanced your horizontal and vertical energy.

Repeat this exercise regularly if the symptoms persist. [This template is not a replacement for any medical attention you may need.]

The Art of Self-Healing

These are some of the healing templates that have been developed over the last 30 years. See next chapter to find out how you can learn more.

Chapter 13
Where to Now?

How do you feel after making your way through all of that! Did you do some or all of the exercises?

Are you wondering where to now?

The power of intuitive healing is in the consistency and focus of your intention.

Yes, you can have great results with an acute problem, but what about when it's a chronic problem. It's similar to breaking a pattern; you need to keep doing the template. What I've noticed is when people learn a template and do the work repeatedly they get really great results.

The more I unpack vibrational healing templates, the more I feel this ground breaking work is the way for future healing protocols.

You can use the healing templates and wisdom in this book to help with your health and wellness.

Here's the thing though, you will need to practice.

The Art of Self-Healing

Sometimes you will feel you aren't getting results and that is not the signal for you to stop. It is the clue to be creative and find another opening from which to tackle the problem.

Doubt

Doubt is going to be your biggest enemy. And yes, it presents itself at the most inappropriate times. Let's look at doubt from another perspective, what if you use doubt as your trigger to re-evaluate your commitment to intuition and following this path.

It is good to question your life philosophy, your intentions, and your beliefs. When you learn you grow, when you grow you let go of old patterns and create new ones. In the letting go, conflict can rise up as resistance to this change.

This quote from Paulo Coelho – *The Devil & Miss Prym* pg 33 illuminates very well the dilemma we experience when faced with change:

> "There are two things that prevent us from achieving our dreams – believing them to be impossible or seeing those dreams made possible by some sudden turn of the wheel of fortune, when you least expected it. For at that moment all our fears suddenly surface. The fear of setting off along a road heading who knows where, the fear of a life full of new challenges, the fear of losing forever everything that is familiar.
>
> People want to change everything and, at the same time, want it all to remain the same."

When you do something new, you are like a baby – a bit wobbly at first. This is when your commitment is tested. When you have to dig deep into your inner well of resources to continue with your development in the face of doubt. This is the time to let your inner knowing shine, not to dull it with the grime of doubt.

Everyone experiences doubt. What you do with it is your yardstick measure.

doubt = invalidation of your intuition

You choose:

Validate your intuition – take action based on your inner knowing.

Invalidate your intuition – don't take the appropriate action and deal with the consequences.

Template for "What to do next"

Working out what to do next is a huge challenge for some and I've experienced this many times myself.

How would you like to have a technique that can help you get an insight into your next move?

This is an extraordinary process which has helped many people get the job of their dreams, create awesome change in their businesses and lives. I encourage you to give this method of determining your next move a good crack. You may be surprised at what happens when you do.

Exercise: What To Do Next

Sit in a quiet space:

- **Imagine** you are walking through a forest.
- Walk down about 10 steps.
- You come to a stream and there are 7 stepping stones – step onto the first stepping stone and a red light shines up – and then the next. Each stone has a different colour – orange, yellow, green, blue, purple, violet.
- You are on the other side of the bank and in front of you is a magnificent door. Walk up to the door – put your hands on the door and keep pushing as they will go straight through.
- Follow your hands with your body and you are in a meeting room.
- There is a table with chairs – nothing else - a door to the right and a

door to the left.

- In front of you is your big chair with buttons on the arm rest – press one of the buttons to open the right hand door and invite the people who will be interviewing you or whom you want a meeting with into the room.
- Ask them to sit down and you interview them. Find out what they want from you to make you an ideal person for the job or whatever you are doing this template for.
- When you are finished asking them questions and interacting with them – thank them for their time and press a button on the left arm of your chair and they leave via the left door.
- You turn around and leave the way you came through the door behind you, go back across the stepping stones and as you step on each stone the colour recedes back into the stone.
- Go up the stairs and back along the path, come all the way back into the room and into your body.
- Become fully present in your body, filling your bones, muscles, organs, bloodstream with the essence of you.
- Take a deep breath in, hold it and gently release it as you come all the way back into the room.

Take note of the information you received on this journey and take the appropriate action you were given insight into.

Different ways you can learn more

In 1984, when I said to God, *"Show me what to do and I'll do it"*, I could not have conceived the extraordinary adventure that was to unfold. I now get to share the wisdom that journey delivered with you.

Head to julielewin.com to further explore The Art of Self-Healing.

※

To finish my story, I have passed my 54th birthday; am happily married to my first husband Frank; have overcome many illnesses beating multiple cancer episodes; found peace, health, happiness and harmony; discovered how to see inside the body and helped many people around the world with this wisdom.

When you have laser focus on a dream, purpose, goal and you are persistent day in day out with achieving that dream, purpose, goal you can do it.

I changed the course of my destiny (if you believe the aura reader), developed exceptional intuition in the process and created a unique healing modality.

What can you do with a dream, persistence and dedication to your goal?

ABOUT THE AUTHOR

Do you have a sense that there is something more that you could do if only you knew how? Is it time for you to listen to you, see real results and say goodbye to your limitations?

In her new book The Art of Self-Healing, Julie Lewin shares her healing modality AreekeerA®. It is a registered modality with the International Institute for Complementary Therapists (IICT). It is easy to learn and can have a profound impact on your health, wellness and life.

Anyone can develop their intuitive healing skills. So can you. Here's what you will discover in this book:

- Intuitive health insight – what is it and how you can do it, too
- How to activate your self-healing resources – transform your pain body yourself
- Read the signposts your body and the environment provide to help you quickly locate the root cause of disease and discomfort in yourself
- Be your own intuitive health detective

Julie Lewin, world renowned Medical Intuitive, Teacher, Speaker, Author, TV and Radio Personality and Founder of AreekeerA®, is passionate about helping people live their full potential – physically, mentally, emotionally and spiritually. Since appearing on 4 episodes of the TV show "The Extraordinary" in 1994 and 1996, Julie is sought after worldwide for her unique intuitive healing skills. Her down to Earth and practical spiritual approach to health and wellness makes you feel safe. www.julielewin.com

NOTES

1. Fiann Ó Nualláin, Interior landscaping in the workplace, benefits to business
2. Rev. Marilyn O'Sullivan, Prayer of Protection, Brisbane, 1987
3. Irvin D Yalom, Love's Executioner
4. John Lennon, song "Imagine"
5. Zen Forum – www.zenforuminternational.org
6. Lucia Capacchione, The Power of Your Other Hand
7. http://jennyhoople.com/blog/how-to-find-your-core-values - sourced on 25/3/13
8. Extract of interview with Drunvalo Melchizedek by Diane Cooper called "Children of the New Dream"
9. Paulo Coelho, "The Devil & Miss Prym" extract from page 33
10. Source: Exercise #15 – Oil pulling http://www.naturalnews.com/043016_oil_pulling_body_detoxification_Ayurvedic_medicine.html

FOOTNOTES

1. http://en.wikipedia.org/wiki/Chakra - 17/2/13
2. David Wilcock, 2012, "The Hidden Science in Lost Civilisations", p167-169
3. http://www.mtstcil.org/skills/stress-definition-1.html - 2/1/13

TEMPLATES

380 Nanometer crystal hut 154
A loved one protection 35
Alimentary canal healing 165
Bubble over house 30
Burn healing 185
Car protection 31
Clunky or crunchy shoulder 189
Cut energy cords 133
DNA codon activation 181
Energy protection egg 28
Flower balancing for anxiety 190
Fluid retention 175
Full body tune up 183
Gallstones remedy 171
Hold hands under running water 133
IBS spasm healing 168
Infection healing 179
Magic blinds 30
Magic mirror cylinder 25
Master cell healing 155
Personal cleansing 18
Prayer of protection 27
Regeneration meditation 150
Shoulder pain release 173
Tips of fingers together 132
Tongue to the roof of the mouth 26, 132

EXERCISES

Access memory 49
Balance emotions with the breath 141
Bowel healing elixir 61
Breath meditation 41
Candle meditation 41
Cleansing your home 19
Cleansing your work environment 20
Creative visualisation 48
Discover your tangible sign for intuition 113
Emotion journal 144
Empath radio dial 98
Eye balm 63
Find your core values 124
Have a confidante 144
How to handle too much empathy 97
How to stay above the amnesia line 88
Journal exercise 78
Left hand / right hand drawing 113
Left hand / right hand writing 115
Magnify hearing 62
Mirror writing 116
Oil pulling 64
Patterned healing water 39
Pay me first 59
Receive 55
Release neck tension 64
Release pain 58
Release stress and anxiety 160
Retreat day 60
Say no 90
Sharing nature's energy meditation 42
Spine stress release 65
Spontaneous visualisation 48
Strengths and weaknesses 86
Technology free time 37
Telepathy exercise 117
Train light meditation 42
Ways to rejuvenate 38
What to do next meditation 195
Write a letter 143

www.ingramcontent.com/pod-product-compliance
Lightning Source LLC
Chambersburg PA
CBHW020649300426
44112CB00007B/299